1,339 QI FACTS

John Lloyd CBE is the creator of QI
and the man who devised *The News Quiz*
and *To the Manor Born* for radio and
Not the Nine O'Clock News, *Spitting Image*
and *Blackadder* for television.
His favourite page is 213.

John Mitchinson, QI's Director of Research,
has been both bookseller and publisher
and looked after authors as diverse as
Haruki Murakami, The Beatles and
a woman who knitted with dog hair.
His favourite page is 26.

James Harkin, QI's Senior Researcher,
has a maths and physics degree, a dark past
as an accountant for a chain of pubs and is
nicknamed 'Turbo' for his phenomenal work rate.
His favourite page is 83.

by John Lloyd, John Mitchinson & James Harkin

1,227 QI FACTS TO BLOW YOUR SOCKS OFF

by John Lloyd & John Mitchinson

THE BOOK OF GENERAL IGNORANCE

THE SECOND BOOK OF GENERAL IGNORANCE

THE BOOK OF ANIMAL IGNORANCE

ADVANCED BANTER: THE QI BOOK OF QUOTATIONS

THE QI BOOK OF THE DEAD

edited by John Lloyd & John Mitchinson

THE QI 'E' ANNUAL

THE QI 'F' ANNUAL

THE QI 'G' ANNUAL

THE QI 'H' ANNUAL

by John Lloyd & Douglas Adams

THE MEANING OF LIFF

THE DEEPER MEANING OF LIFF

by John Lloyd & Jon Canter

AFTERLIFF

A QUITE INTERESTING BOOK

1,339 QI FACTS

TO MAKE YOUR JAW DROP

Compiled by
John Lloyd, John Mitchinson
& James Harkin

with the QI Elves
Anne Miller, Andrew Hunter Murray,
Anna Ptaszynski & Alex Bell

FABER & FABER

First published in 2013
by Faber and Faber Ltd
Bloomsbury House
74–77 Great Russell Street
London wc1b 3da

Typeset by Palindrome
Printed in England by CPI Group (UK) Ltd,
Croydon cr0 4yy

A CIP record for this book
is available from the British Library

isbn 978–0–571–30894–1

2 4 6 8 10 9 7 5 3 1

Contents

Introduction

Truth is the daughter of search.
ARABIC PROVERB

When we came to write our first volume of facts – *1,227 Quite Interesting Facts To Blow Your Socks Off* – we set ourselves the modest goal of producing 1,000 nuggets of information that seemed to us unforgettable. We pooled ten years of extraordinary comparisons (there are 1,000 times as many bacteria in your gut as there are stars in the Milky Way); astonishing statistics (a single male produces enough sperm in two weeks to impregnate every fertile woman on the planet); unexpected truths (the Bible is the most shoplifted book in America) and memorable absurdities (Richard Gere's middle name is Tiffany), and then counted up what we had. It turned out we had a file of 1,227 facts, which seemed both more interesting and more appropriate than the 1,000 we'd originally targeted.

In the course of editing and arranging that material we discovered something surprising: the facts seemed to have a mind of their own. Far from being inert pieces of trivia, they behaved much more like molecules, bristling with energy and a desire to form strong attractions with other facts to make longer and more meaningful sequences. All we had to do was keep trying the best combinations.

As well as being deeply satisfying, this process of fact-matching also meant we needed to create a much deeper pool of truth in which to dip our editorial spoon. And before we'd finished, we realised that the new pile of strange and wonderful facts we hadn't been able to sequence was already forming the core of a new book.

We always tell our researchers that to find the best stuff, all you have to do is to look longer and more closely. That has been our guiding principle in compiling this second volume. Once you are in the Fact Zone, everywhere you look, astonishing *new* facts seem to wave and demand inclusion. We hope you find the combinations that we – and they – have made as satisfying as last time.

And, to adapt a line of Groucho Marx, if you don't like them – well, we've got others.

JOHN LLOYD, JOHN MITCHINSON
& JAMES HARKIN

*Facts are to the mind
what food is to the body.*
EDMUND BURKE (1729–1797)

There are 1,339 bank branches
in Peru.

There are 1,339 outdoor sculptures
in Texas.

There are 1,339 Christian churches
in Wenzhou, China.

There are 1,339 illegal factories
in Samanabad, Pakistan.

Pakistan means
'Land of the Pure'
in Urdu.

The most commonly used
word for 'detergent' in Urdu
is 'Surf'.

It is illegal in China
to show TV ads for
haemorrhoid cream
at mealtimes.

One in seven UK banknotes
carries traces of
anal bacteria.

Babies are born
with no bacteria
in their bodies.

The word 'infant'
is from the Latin for
'unable to speak'.

'Bow-wow', 'Ding-dong' and 'Pooh-pooh'
are all names for different theories
about the origin of language.

Winnie the Pooh's
real name is
Edward Bear.

The offspring of
a polar bear and a grizzly bear
is called a pizzly bear.

A baby pterosaur
is called a flapling.

Cockroaches
appeared 120 million years
before the dinosaurs.

The Himalayas were formed
25 million years after the last dinosaur
died out.

All the mountains
on Saturn's moon Titan
are named after peaks in
The Lord of the Rings.

J. R. R. Tolkien and Adolf Hitler
both fought at
the battle of the Somme.

During Hitler's years in power,
Mein Kampf was given away free
to every newly-wed couple.

Mussolini described *Mein Kampf* as
'a boring tome that I have never
been able to read'.

The most-read publication in the UK
is *Tesco* magazine.

A pint of milk in a supermarket
can contain milk from
over a thousand different cows.

The average Briton consumes
8 cows, 36 sheep and 36 pigs
in a lifetime.

A raw carrot
is still alive when you eat it.

Half the food
produced in the world
is left to rot.

Every hour,
the UK produces enough waste
to fill the Albert Hall.

If the Albert Hall were a freezer,
it could hold all the galaxies
in the visible universe
if they were the size of
frozen peas.

Howard Hughes
kept a ruler in his hotel room
to measure any peas he ordered,
sending back those that
were 'too big'.

CCD
(canine compulsive disorder)
is OCD for dogs.

In German,
'Dogging'
is jogging with your dog.

Bloodhounds' noses
are 100 million times more sensitive
than human noses.

Astronauts' helmets
contain a small piece of Velcro
so they can scratch their noses.

According to
Velcro's official website,
there is no such thing as Velcro.

Splenda was an insecticide
that became a sweetener
when an assistant misheard
an order to 'test' it as 'taste' it.

Samsung's
first product was
dried fish.

Wrigley's
originally made
soap.

Chewing gum costs
3p a stick to buy
but 10p a blob
to clean off the pavement.

Second Street is the most common
street name in the USA.
First Street is the
third most common.

The oldest bridge in Paris
is the Pont Neuf,
or 'New Bridge'.

More than half
the fish in the USA
labelled as tuna
is not tuna.

Half of all animal and plant species
live in only one country and
nowhere else.

Half of British adults
don't believe in evolution.

Most clams begin life as males,
but half of them
turn female when older.

The Green Zone Golf Club
is on the border of Finland and Sweden:
half the holes are in one country
and half in the other.

The first woman to play golf was
Mary Queen of Scots.

Agatha Christie
was a keen surfer.

George W. Bush
was a college cheerleader.

Bruce Lee
was Hong Kong's 1958
cha-cha dance champion.

The oldest dance
still performed is
the Austrian shoe-slapping dance.

The oldest animal ever found
was a 405-year-old Icelandic clam.
It was killed by researchers
trying to work out its age.

Women
look their oldest
at 3.30 p.m. on Wednesdays.

Nudiustertian means
'relating to the day before yesterday'.

The word 'journey'
is from the French *journée*
and once meant the distance
one could walk in a day.

The Swahili for 'journey'
is *safari*.

The *Express*, the *Telegraph*,
the *Economist*, the *Times*,
the *Star* and the *Independent*
were all London-based stagecoaches
in the 1830s.

The Solar System is travelling
round the galaxy at more than
half a million miles per hour.

A Manx shearwater
flies over 5 million miles
in its lifetime.

Zugunruhe
is the restlessness of caged birds
in the migration season.

Urban birds have learned to line
their nests with cigarette butts.
Nicotine is a powerful insecticide
that wards off mites, lice and fleas.

The nectar of citrus plants
contains caffeine
to attract bees.

David Cameron
used to be president of the
Oxfordshire Bee Keepers' Association.

Pannage
was a tax on keeping
pigs in royal forests
that was paid in pigs.

Henry VIII
put a tax on beards in 1535,
but made sure his own was exempt.

King David I of Scotland
gave tax rebates to subjects
with good table manners.

William the Conqueror
had been in England for a fortnight
before the battle of Hastings.

King John
was named 'Softsword'
for his feeble military activities.

In the Hundred Years War,
the French called the English 'godons'
because they were always shouting
'God damn'.

Lalochezia is
using swearing to
relieve stress or pain.

The words
proctalgia, proctodynia,
pygalgia and *rectalgia*
all mean 'pain in the backside'.

In Exodus 33:23,
God shows Moses his backside:
'And I will take away mine hand,
and thou shalt see my back parts.'

St Martin of Tours
exorcised people
by shoving his arm down their throats
and forcing the devil out of their anus.

500,000 Italians
visit an exorcist every year.

'The devil's port-gate'
was an Elizabethan euphemism
for the vagina.

In the 18th century,
'bum-fodder' and 'arse-wisp'
both meant toilet paper.

On an average day,
Britons spend
14 hours and 39 minutes
sitting down.

Before dentists' chairs were invented,
the patient's head was clenched
between the surgeon's knees.

The electric chair
was invented by a dentist.

The first guillotine
was built by a harpsichord maker.

The first private detective agency
was started by a criminal.

Speed dating
was the brainchild of a rabbi.

The quickest possible
round-the-world flight time
by commercial airline
is 44 hours.

The remains of birds
hit by aeroplanes
are known as
'snarge'.

80% of plane crashes
occur in the
first three or last eight
minutes of a flight.

Only 5%
of the world's population
has ever been on an aeroplane.

Before Amy Johnson flew solo
from Britain to Australia,
the furthest she had flown was
from Hendon to Hull.

Nearly half of all airline pilots
admit they have
fallen asleep on the job.

The first man-made object in space
was the German V2 rocket.

Russian cosmonauts
routinely took guns into space
in case re-entry landed them
in the Siberian wilderness.

In 1905,
the city of Birmingham
banned rifle shooting in pubs.

The gun laws
in Tombstone, Arizona,
are less strict today
than they were at the time of
the OK Corral.

In Kennesaw, Georgia,
gun ownership is required by law.

There is only one gun shop in Mexico:
90% of the country's firearms
are smuggled in from the USA.

On 18th February 1913,
Pedro Lascuráin resigned
as president of Mexico
after holding office
for less than an hour.

The Marianas Trench in the Pacific
is so deep that a coin
dropped into it from the surface
will take more than an hour
to reach the bottom.

Spiders can survive for hours underwater
by entering a self-induced coma.

A bite from the
Brazilian wandering spider
results in an erection
that lasts for several hours.

In Britain,
spiders outnumber people
by more than 500,000 to 1.

The Natural History Museum
in London has 22,000 drawers
filled with beetles.

If dung beetles
disappeared from the plains of Africa,
its human inhabitants would be
up to their waists in excrement
within a month.

Until biological softener
was invented in 1908,
the standard way to soften leather
was to smear it with dog faeces.

Entrance to the Tower of London
used to be free if you
brought a dog or a cat
to feed to the lions.

The Eiffel Tower
was scheduled to be
pulled down
in 1909.

The Louvre
was built in 1190
as a defence against Viking raids.

The Statue of Liberty
wears size 879 shoes.

Charles II of England
wore stilettos to his coronation.

Samantha Cameron is the
great-great-great-great-great-great-great-
granddaughter of Charles II's mistress,
Nell Gwyn.

David Cameron is a
great-great-great-great-great-grandson
of King William IV.

At least 170 civil servants
in the UK are paid more than
the prime minister.

The House of Commons chamber
can only seat three-quarters
of the country's MPs.

In July 2013,
more people in Britain
believed in ghosts than
supported the Labour Party.

More people in Britain
describe their religion as 'Jedi Knight'
than are members of the Tory party.

Since the 2001 census,
the number of people in Britain
claiming to be Jedi
has fallen by more than half.

Harrison Ford used to be a carpenter.
He was fitting a door when
George Lucas asked him
to audition for *Star Wars*.

Ozzy Osbourne
worked in a morgue
and a slaughterhouse.

Warren Beatty
worked as a rat-catcher.

Danny DeVito
is a qualified hairdresser.

The average woman
has 150 different hairstyles
in her lifetime.

In 1950,
7% of American women
dyed their hair.
In 2013, it was 75%.

Healthy hair
can stretch by 50%
when wet.

Your hair grows
more quickly when
you're anticipating sex.

Plants grow more quickly
if you talk to them
in a Geordie accent.

Magnolias are the oldest
surviving flowering plants;
they first appeared
100 million years ago.

The rarest flower in Britain
is the lady's slipper orchid:
a single specimen lives on
a golf course in Lancashire
under police surveillance.

The symbol of the
Alzheimer's Society of Canada
is the forget-me-not.

The existence of
photographic memory has
never been scientifically proven.

A decapitated
planarian flatworm
grows a new brain
complete with all its old memories.

A human liver
can grow back even after
75% of it has been removed.

95% of all avocados on sale today
are descended from one tree
grown by a Milwaukee postman in 1926.

In French, *avocat* means
both 'lawyer' and 'avocado'.

In German, *Strauss* means
both 'ostrich' and 'bunch of flowers'.

In Norwegian, *pålegg* is
'anything that could conceivably
be put in a sandwich'.

In Old Norse, *kveis* meant
'uneasiness after debauchery'.

Gambrinous means
'being full of beer'.

Hops contain antioxidants,
but you'd have to drink
118 gallons of beer a day
to see any health benefit.

French wrestler
André the Giant
once drank 119 beers
in six hours.

In 1876,
the Munich Health Department
ruled that breastfeeding women
only needed to drink
two pints of beer a day.

Edgar Allan Poe's poem 'The Raven'
was originally going to be about
a talking parrot.

The last speaker
of the Amazonian Ature language
was a parrot.

Parrots
can live for 80 years.

There are whales alive today
that were born before
Moby-Dick was written
in 1851.

If a dead whale is found
on a British beach,
the head belongs to the king
and the tail to the queen.

The first two police officers
sworn into the Metropolitan Police
were both later sacked for
'drunkenness in the streets'.

The 'de-militarised' zone
between North and South Korea
is the world's most militarised zone.

The 1784 'Kettle War'
between the Netherlands
and the Holy Roman Empire
involved only a single shot.
It hit a kettle.

21% of British households
don't possess a kettle.

One in eight British adults
owns a onesie.

Two-thirds of British children aged 5 to 13
can work a DVD player,
but fewer than half
can tie their shoelaces.

60% of British meals
are eaten in front of the TV.

Early BBC TV
showed pictures and sound alternately:
they only had one transmitter
so couldn't do both at the same time.

Until the 1920s,
television was also known as
Hear-seeing, Seeing by Wireless,
Optiphone, Farscope
and the Electric Telescope.

'TV dinners' were so-called because
the compartments resembled
the screen and knobs
on an old-style round-cornered TV.

Rounded corners on electronic devices
have been patented
by Apple.

Nokia once made gas masks:
the Finnish army used them
until 1995.

The French company Bich
changed its name to Bic
to stop people in
English-speaking countries
pronouncing it 'bitch'.

Play-Doh
was originally designed as
wallpaper cleaner.

The first bubblegum
produced bubbles that
had to be removed from the face
with turpentine.

James I of England
only ever washed
the tips of his fingers.

Louis XIII of France
wasn't bathed until he was
almost seven.

According to a passenger from Sudan,
the first London Underground trains
smelt 'like crocodile breath'.

The air in London
is cleaner now than at any time
since the 16th century.

In the 16th century,
Britain had one pub
for every 200 people.

At any one time,
45 million people in the world
are drunk.

Hangovers cost the US economy
more than $220 billion
in lost productivity each year.

A popular Roman hangover cure
was deep-fried canary.

Pliny the Elder
advised tying a fox's genitals
to the brow
to cure headaches.

Chopin whistled
or played chords on the piano
when he had trouble urinating.

Giving Prozac to a snail
renders it unable
to stick to surfaces.

Viagra was developed
to treat angina.

Fatal heart attacks
were unknown before 1900.
The first medical description of one
in Britain was in 1925.

The human heart is not
on the left-hand side of the body,
it's in the middle.

Each time a fertile man's heart beats,
he makes 1,500 new sperm.

Over a lifetime,
the human heart pumps enough blood
to fill a football stadium.

In 1903,
the three largest
sports stadiums in the world
were all in Glasgow.

The pregnancy of the
frilled shark lasts for three years,
the longest in nature.

The tuatara,
a New Zealand reptile
that pre-dates the dinosaurs,
has three eyes.

Babies have three times
as many taste buds as adults.

Squid
taste with their
tentacles.

The Chinese fruit
Siraitia grosvenorii
is 300 times sweeter than sugar.

The principal killer of elephants
in American zoos
is obesity.

North Americans account for
less than a sixteenth of
the world's people,
but more than a third
of their weight.

Kunga cake
is an East African food
made from millions of
crushed midges.

The star-nosed mole
can identify and eat
an insect quicker than
you can read the word 'mole'.

Flamingo tongues
were a delicacy
in ancient Rome.

A tiger's tongue is so rough
that if it licked your hand
it would draw blood.

More is known
about the behaviour of
big cats in Africa than
that of domestic cats in Britain.

In 17th-century England,
effigies of Guy Fawkes
were stuffed with live cats
to make the figure scream as it burned.

The Kattenstoet
was a medieval festival in Belgium
in which cats were thrown
from the town's belfry.

In 1879, the Belgian city of Liège
commissioned 37 cats
to deliver mail to nearby villages.
The project was a complete failure.

John Lennon and Paul McCartney
both had cats named Jesus.

The Beatles classic 'Yesterday'
was originally titled
'Scrambled Eggs'.

'I'm a Poached Egg'
is a love song by
George Gershwin.

Albert Einstein
claimed his second-best idea
was to boil his eggs in his soup,
thus saving on washing-up.

The Moon is shaped like an egg:
it only looks round because
the big end points towards Earth.

The coldest known place
in the Solar System
is in a crater at
the north pole of the Moon.

Oymyakon in Russia
is the coldest inhabited town on Earth:
its only hotel has no hot water
and an outside toilet.

Between 2010 and 2013,
the London Fire Brigade rescued
18 children with their heads
stuck in toilet seats.

After just four moves
in a game of chess, there are
318,979,564,000 possibilities
for the layout of the board.

The 1978 chess final at
HM Prison Wormwood Scrubs was
between 'Moors Murderer' Ian Brady
and disgraced MP John Stonehouse.

In 1913,
Hitler, Stalin, Trotsky, Tito,
Freud, Jung and Wittgenstein
were all living in Vienna.

Dublin, Glasgow, London,
Petroleum, Coal, Wax
Goforth, Stay and Jump
are all towns in Kentucky.

The Irish pub
furthest from Dublin
is Waxy O'Shea's in
Invercargill, New Zealand.

Villages in County Durham
include Pity Me and
No Place.

There are six villages
in France called Silly,
12 called Billy
and two called Prat.

There are 11 places in Utah
called Mollys Nipple, Mollies Nipple or
Molleys Nipple.

Female giant jumping rats
have four nipples:
two in the armpits
and two in the groin.

Buzz
is Arabic for 'nipple'.

Dad
is Albanian for 'babysitter'.

Waterponie
is Afrikaans for 'jet-ski'.

10,000 horses were killed
at the battle of Waterloo.

The first Skyscraper
was a particularly tall horse
that won the Epsom Derby
in 1789.

Snickers bars are named after
a horse owned by the Mars company.

Humans have one more bone
in their bodies than horses.

Human bone is
four times stronger
than concrete.

Your brain cells live longer
than any other cells
in your body.

You have taste receptors
in your lungs.

The Cornish for 'heart'
is *colon*.

Hands evolved
before arms.

After a double hand transplant,
right-handed patients
can become left-handed.

Mothers over 40
are twice as likely
to have left-handed children
as women in their 20s.

Until the early 20th century,
left-handedness in a wife
was grounds for divorce in Japan.

The Japanese for 'poverty'
is *bimbo*.

Raicho,
meaning 'thunderbird',
is Japanese for the
rock ptarmigan or
snow chicken.

Chicken, Alaska,
was going to be called
Ptarmigan, Alaska,
but no one could agree
on the spelling.

Alaska is the
northernmost, westernmost
and easternmost state
in the USA.

'Alaska strawberries'
was 19th-century slang for
'dried beans'.

Empress Isabelle of Bavaria
bathed in strawberry juice.

In the Azerbaijani town of Naftalan,
people bathe in crude oil
to ease joint pains.

Male eland antelopes
let other males know
how tough they are
by clicking their knees.

Anglerfish
have black-lined stomachs
to stop their insides
giving them away
after they eat something
luminous.

The longest recorded flight
of a domestic chicken
lasted 13 seconds.

The highest-ever jump
by a rabbit
measured 3 feet 3 inches.

A rabbit was the only casualty
of the first bomb in
the Second World War
to fall on British soil.

95% of baby rabbits
don't survive beyond
their first six months.

In three years,
two mating rabbits
can theoretically produce
33 million relatives.

The world's biggest rabbit,
Ralph from East Sussex,
costs £50 a week to feed.

Earmuffs
were invented by
a 13-year-old.

Within seven years of their invention,
60% of the US population
owned boomboxes.

A collection of boomerangs
and a Z-bed were found in
Tutankhamun's tomb.

Tutankhamun died
of a broken leg.

Some whales are born
with a small leg
protruding from their body.

Whales have hip bones,
which means they must
have once left the oceans,
grown legs, decided they didn't like it
and gone back into the sea again.

The barstools on
Aristotle Onassis's yacht
were upholstered with
whales' foreskins.

Moby-Dick
was based on a real sperm whale
called Mocha Dick.

Geronimo's real name
was Goyathlay,
meaning
'he who yawns'.

Yawning cools your brain,
like a fan cools the inside
of a computer.

Babies yawn in the womb;
they also swallow, stretch and hiccup.

Babies up to the age of six months
can swallow and breathe
at the same time.

Pandiculation is
yawning and stretching
at the same time.

There is enough tissue
in a human lung
to cover a tennis court.

There is enough carbon
in your body
to make 9,000 pencils.

You lose a pound of carbon
in weight every night
just from breathing.

Diamonds boil
at 4,027°C.

−40° Celsius
and −40° Fahrenheit
are the same temperature.

15 °C is
the highest temperature
ever recorded in Antarctica.

There are 300 lakes
beneath Antarctica
that are kept from freezing by
the warmth of the Earth's core.

Husky dogs have been banned
from Antarctica since 1994.

When Roald Amundsen
travelled to the South Pole,
he ate his huskies
on the way back.

Only one dog
has ever been to both
the North and South Poles.

During the 1962 World Cup,
a dog ran onto the pitch
and urinated on Jimmy Greaves.

Russian cosmonauts urinate
on the right rear wheel of the bus
taking them to the space shuttle
to bring themselves luck.

The 'I'm Feeling Lucky' button
on Google costs the company
$110 million a year
in lost ad revenue.

In 2006, a man named Ronald Man
had a heart attack and crashed his car;
the impact worked like a defibrillator
and restarted his heart.

James Dean's
last appearance on film
before his fatal car crash in 1955
was in a road-safety commercial.

In 1895,
the only two cars in Ohio
crashed into each other.

The odds of hitting
two holes-in-one
in the same round of golf
are 67 million to one.

Mo Farah,
Sir Roger Bannister, Sir Chris Hoy,
Jason Kenny and Sir Steve Redgrave
were all born on March 23rd.

Moses, Raphael, Arnold Bennett,
Captain Oates and Ingrid Bergman
all died on their birthdays.

The ancient city of Alexandria
was built so that the sun
shone down the main street
on Alexander the Great's birthday.

Galileo was born on the day that
Michelangelo died.

People who die of old age
are more likely to die at 11 a.m.
than at any other time.

Three US presidents died on 4th July:
John Adams and Thomas Jefferson in 1826,
and James Monroe five years later.

Between April and July 1776,
US states issued
more than 90 different
Declarations of Independence.

John Adams,
2nd president of the USA,
took up smoking
at the age of eight.

John Tyler,
10th president of the USA,
was born in 1790 but
two of his grandsons are still alive.

When George W. Bush,
43rd president of the USA,
arrived in the White House, he found
the Clinton administration had removed
the 'W' keys from all the computers.

'President Clinton of the USA'
is an anagram of
'to copulate, he finds interns'.

In 1999,
the president of Niger was
Major Wanke.

In 1939,
835 sheep were killed by
a single lightning strike in Utah.

The best way to
avoid being struck by lightning
is to crouch down away from any trees
with your bottom sticking up in the air.

Blowing air up
an armadillo's bottom
causes it to leap three feet into the air.

Air trapped inside hedgehogs
can make them blow up like a balloon.
They should be carefully
deflated with a syringe
before they burst.

The Victorians
kept hedgehogs
in their kitchens to
control cockroaches.

If a cockroach touches a person,
it immediately runs away
and washes itself.

Rats urinate on food
to mark it as edible.

Monkeys urinate
on themselves
to attract a mate.

An ostrich can
kill a lion
with a single blow.

Being attacked by an ostrich
left Johnny Cash with
an addiction to painkillers.

Early Arabic texts
refer to cannabis as
'the bush of understanding'
and 'the shrub of emotion'.

In 1850, cannabis was used in the USA
to treat tetanus, typhus, cholera, rabies,
dysentery, alcoholism, anthrax,
leprosy, snake bites, tonsillitis
and insanity.

Ketamine was the
most commonly used anaesthetic
during the Vietnam War.

A Macedonian soldier from 300 BC
was more likely to survive treatment
for a wound than a British soldier
at Sebastopol in 1854.

Patients admitted to hospital
at the weekend
are 40% more likely to die
than those admitted
during the working week.

A human being can survive
for nine seconds at 1,000 °C
without suffering lasting damage.

Since 1940,
157 people have fallen from planes
without parachutes and survived.

Since 1990,
more people have been killed by
sandcastles than by sharks.

Shark Bay, Australia,
is now called 'Safety Beach'.
It changed its name
to attract tourists.

Kangaroo Island was named in 1802
by Matthew Flinders after he and his crew
slaughtered 31 kangaroos there
and made them into soup.

At birth, a kangaroo
is smaller than a cherry.

Because opossums have forked penises,
early naturalists thought males mated
with the female's nose.

A *renifleur* is someone
who gets sexual pleasure
from smells.

The human nose
can distinguish between
over 10,000 different smells.

Rhinotillexomania
is the scientific term for being
unable to stop picking your nose.

It is impossible to hum
while holding your nose.

Humpback whales
can sing non-stop
for 20 hours.

Nightingales
can remember
over 200 different songs.

The fastest known muscle
in nature is found in the
throats of songbirds.

The superb fairy wren
teaches its chicks to sing
while they are still in the egg.

Ludo
was invented
in ancient India.

Jenga means 'to build'
in Swahili.

Chinese checkers
was invented in
Germany.

Samuel Taylor Coleridge
invented the sport of
rock-climbing.

William Webb Ellis
died in France, completely unaware
he had been credited with
the invention of rugby.

The French Vichy government
banned rugby league because
they considered it
a communist sport.

Rugby School's
first official rugby kit in 1871
included a bow tie.

The Nazi uniforms
were designed by
Hugo Boss.

When Josef Mengele
fled to Argentina
he went through customs
with several suitcases full of
human body parts.

Iran is the
only country in the world
where it is legal to sell your kidneys.

In Alabama, it is illegal
to recommend shades of paint
without a licence.

The Knights Templar's
most important rule was
to avoid kissing women.

The ancient Greek city of Megara
held a version of the Olympic Games
which included a kissing contest.
Only boys were allowed to enter.

PE teachers were originally banned
from the modern Olympics because
they were professionals.

At the 1908
Olympic Games in London,
Great Britain won
gold, silver and bronze
in the tug of war.

The Kalenjin people of Kenya
make up 0.05% of the world's population
but have won almost 50% of its major
distance-running events since 1980.

The fastest 100 metres
run by an eight-year-old today
would have won bronze
at the 1896 Olympics.

The 1988 Olympics
included the sport of
solo synchronised swimming.

Polar bears
can swim 60 miles
without stopping.

An ostrich
could run the
London Marathon
in 45 minutes.

A garden snail
would take three years and two months
to make its way from
John O'Groats to Land's End.

Light
travels from
John O'Groats to Land's End
in 0.00469 seconds.

8,000 years ago,
Britain had so many trees
that a squirrel could go from
John O'Groats to Land's End
without touching the ground.

Nemophilia
is the love of spending time
in forests.

Two out of three trees
in the world are
dangerously parched.

The only way to tell if trees
are short of water
is to record the sounds they make:
the thirstier they are,
the louder they get.

Different branches
on the same ash tree can be
male, female or both at once.

Oysters change their sex
up to four times a year.

Fruit bats enjoy fellatio.

Men are more likely to
die during sex if they're
cheating on their wives.

More than one-third of
men using dating sites
are already married.

More than one-third of
married Canadians
sleep in separate rooms.

Ptolemy VII married
his sister Cleopatra II,
who was also his brother's widow.
So his wife was not only his sister
but his sister-in-law.

Einstein, Rachmaninoff, Darwin,
H. G. Wells and Edgar Allan Poe
all married their first cousins.

When filling in forms,
Agatha Christie
always gave her occupation as
'married woman'.

90% of the world's
teenage mothers aged 16 to 19
are married.

In London,
women over 40
are giving birth at
twice the rate of teenagers.

In Mexican slang,
to 'mother' something is to wreck it,
anything that 'has no mother' is very cool,
and 'mothers!' means 'whoops!'

In Korean, there are
no words for 'brother' or 'sister',
but there are words for
an older or younger brother,
and an older or younger sister.

Having a younger brother or sister
can increase your blood pressure
by more than 5%.

It would take
1.2 million mosquitoes,
each sucking once,
to completely drain
the average human of blood.

A midge
beats its wings
62,750 times a minute.

It takes a male flea
six to eight hours
to unfold all the different parts
of its penis.

Woodlice
have 14 legs.

The vampire spider
is attracted to the smell
of human feet.

Mice
enjoy the smell
of marijuana.

The Japanese word *kareishu*
describes the smell of
old people.

Moths can smell one another
from seven miles away.

The faint trace
of perfume left in the wake
of a passing person is known as
sillage.

In 2007, the makers of Stilton
marketed Eau de Stilton,
a perfume to 'recreate the
earthy and fruity aroma'
of the cheese.

A 'cheeseling'
is a small cheese.

'Cheeselips'
is another name for woodlice:
they were once used
to curdle milk.

A glass of milk
left in the Lut Desert in Iran
will not go off:
the heat is so intense
it kills all the bacteria.

All Neanderthals were
lactose intolerant.

Lee Pearson,
winner of ten Paralympic golds
for dressage,
is allergic to horses.

Pigs suffer from anorexia.

There were fewer than 50 restaurants
in Paris before the 1789 Revolution;
by 1814 there were more than 3,000.

The first Indian restaurant in the UK
opened 50 years before
the first fish-and-chip shop.

The oldest known English cookbook
is called the *Forme of Cury*.

An English person from 2013
could not understand
an English person from 1300
without a translator.

In the 14th century,
a high-spirited person
was known as a
'great-willy'.

Cumbria has villages called
Great Snoring and Great Fryup,
and a hill called
Great Cockup.

Fletcher Christian
and William Wordsworth
were at school together in
Cockermouth, Cumbria.

Wordsworth
had no sense of smell.

Before sending his six-year-old son,
Auberon, to boarding school,
Evelyn Waugh threatened
to change the family name to
Stinkbottom.

Daniel Defoe changed his name
from Daniel Foe in order to sound
more upmarket.

Holly Golightly
from *Breakfast at Tiffany's*
was originally going to be called
Connie Gustafson.

James Bond was originally going
to be called James Secretan.

Margaret Thatcher
was offered passport number 007
but she turned it down.

Brendan O'Carroll,
star of *Mrs Brown's Boys*,
was once Mrs Thatcher's butler.

In the 19th century,
a five-foot six-inch footman
cost £20 a year,
while a full six-footer
would set you back £40.

When they reach
a height of 100 metres,
trees stop growing leaves.

Ten trees were needed
to make the paper to
print the 2013 report
on the environmental impact
of the British HS2 rail scheme.

The British Standards Institution
has a 5,000 word report
on the correct way
to make a cup of tea.

When Swindon station opened in 1840,
all the trains passing through it
had to stop for a ten-minute tea break.

British soldiers
in the First World War
had a tea ration
of six pints a day.

Turning up
the music in a bar by 22%
makes people drink
26% faster.

To 'dibble' is
to drink like a duck,
lifting your head
after each sip.

Lifting your head
on a neutron star
would use more energy
than climbing Mount Everest.

The energy burned off
by the average footballer
in a single match is
equivalent to 15 Jaffa Cakes.

Boys' GCSE results
dip by almost half a grade
in World Cup and
European Championship years.

60% of Premier League footballers
go bankrupt
within five years
of retirement.

Somebody in the UK
is declared bankrupt
every 50 seconds.

Plutomania
is the delusion
that one is immensely rich.

Hewlett-Packard printer ink
is 20 times more expensive
than 2003 vintage
Dom Pérignon champagne.

It is 14 million times cheaper
to store 1GB of data
on a hard drive
than it was in 1981.

There are 2,436
millionaire bankers in the UK,
compared to 170 in Germany
and 162 in France.

The best credit profiles in the UK
are held by men named Brian
and women called Helen.

Julius Caesar
had two sisters,
both called Julia.

Karl and Jenny Marx
named all four
of their daughters
Jenny.

George Foreman has five sons
called George, George Jr, George III,
George IV, George V and George VI,
and a daughter called Georgetta.

Emlyn Hughes's son
is called Emlyn
and his daughter,
Emma-Lynn.

Almost half of newly hatched storks
abandon their nest to look for
a foster parent who might
feed them better.

At least 60% of species on Earth
are parasites.

There are ten times more
bacterial cells in your body
than human ones.

The average human navel
contains 67 different
species of bacteria.

Omphalodium is
another name
for tummy button.

Michelangelo was called a heretic
for giving Adam a belly button
on the Sistine Chapel ceiling.

Rembrandt's
The Night Watch
was so over-restored in the 1940s
it was nicknamed
The Day Watch.

Edvard Munch's
The Scream
is based on a Peruvian mummy
he saw in a Paris museum.

The Louvre
has a naked version
of the *Mona Lisa*,
painted by one of Da Vinci's pupils.

Victor Hugo made
detailed erotic drawings
of all the women
he slept with.

The most expensive sex position
offered by ancient Greek prostitutes
was called *keles*, 'the racehorse'.

Buckingham Palace
is built on the site
of a brothel.

When Queen Victoria arrived in 1837,
there were no bathrooms in
Buckingham Palace.

The word 'palace' comes from
the Palatine Hill in Rome,
where the emperors lived.

The Roman emperor Elagabalus
invented a whoopee cushion
which he used at dinner parties.

Whoopi Goldberg
got her nickname from her
childhood flatulence.

Laurel and Hardy are known as
Dick and Doof in Germany
and Gog and Cokke
in Denmark.

In 1379,
more than 600 years ago,
a baby girl in Yorkshire
was christened Diot Coke.

The Mayan calendar had 18 months,
including 'Pop', 'Zip', 'Zac', 'Mac'
and 'Moan'.

The Comper Mouse, Currie Wot,
Dart Kitten, English Electric Wren,
Luton Minor, Thruxton Jackaroo,
Pobjoy Pirate, Sopwith Grasshopper
and Watkinson Dingbat are all
names of early British aeroplanes.

Aerodontia is
the branch of dentistry
dealing with problems
caused by flying.

Human teeth can detect
a grain of sand
1/2,500 of an inch
in diameter.

Carp have teeth
in their throats.

A blue whale's throat
is the same diameter
as its navel:
about the size of a side plate.

The krill eaten
by a blue whale every day
weigh as much as
40,000 cheeseburgers.

One krill is no longer
than your little finger,
but their swarms are so big
they can be seen from space.

An astronaut is someone who
flies aircraft higher
than 50 miles above sea level.

When Skylab burned up
in Earth's atmosphere in 1979,
the government of Western Australia
fined NASA $400 for littering.
The fine was eventually paid in 2009.

In the USA,
one-third of the domestic waste
sent to landfill
is grass clippings.

Five species of grass
account for half the calories
in the human diet.

Americans eat
10 billion doughnuts
every year.

Obese drivers
are almost twice as likely
to die in a car accident.

Car doors injure
around 600 cyclists
in the UK every year.

Tolstoy had
his first cycling lesson
at 67.

Elgar had a bicycle called
'Mr Phoebus'.

The Arabic word
for a hamster
translates as
'Mr Saddlebags'.

Rodents prefer peanut butter
to cheese.

The world's largest rodent
was a Venezuelan guinea pig
the size of a buffalo.

The world's largest invertebrate
was *Arthropleura*, a ten-foot millipede
that lived in prehistoric Scotland.

The bird with the largest vocabulary
was Puck the Budgie, who died in 1998.
He knew 1,728 words,
the same as a four-year-old child.

The recently extinct
Ubykh language of southern Russia
had 84 consonants
but only two vowels.

The Sedang language
of Laos and Vietnam
has more than 50 vowel sounds.

Oaia aia e a ei
is a Romanian sentence
made only of vowels. It means
'That sheep is hers.'

Vowel-schmowel:
the practice of adding a
rhyming word beginning with sch-
to another is called
'shm-reduplication'.

We dot our 'i's,
but Shakespeare
'tittled' his.

The poet A. E. Housman
kept a notebook in which he jotted down
insults and unpleasant remarks that
occurred to him.

'Son-of-a-bitch stew'
was a cowboy dish made from
the internal organs of a whole cow
and an onion.

Sob Lake in Canada began life as
'Son of a Bitch Lake'.
It was named after a trapper
who had a log cabin on its shore.

Jellyfish Lake
in the Philippines
contains more than
13 million jellyfish.

Rudyard Kipling
got his name from
Rudyard Lake, Staffordshire,
the place where his parents met.

Fish in polluted lakes
lose their sense of smell.

Sunbathing on the shore of
Lake Karachai in Russia
for one hour can give you
a fatal dose of radiation.

There is one Kalashnikov in circulation
for every 70 people on Earth.

IKEA sells one bookcase
somewhere in the world
every ten seconds.

Heinz sells
two sachets of ketchup
each year for every person
on Earth.

Heinz baked beans
were first sold in Britain
at Fortnum & Mason,
as an exclusive luxury
imported from America.

Every Heinz baked bean
passes through a laser beam
to check that it is
the right colour.

The first laser was said to have
the power of one 'Gillette'
as it could burn through
a single razor blade.

In the first seven years
after it opened in 2001,
only one company traded on
the Cameroon stock exchange.

The central European republic
of Carpatho-Ruthenia existed
for just one day, in 1939.

There is only one
Jewish citizen
in Afghanistan.

There is only one
mention of sneezing
in the Bible.

The Russian village of Kozino
has only one resident,
a 76-year-old woman
called Rimma.

The Andamanese language
has only two words for numbers:
they mean 'one' and
'more than one'.

More than 800 languages
are spoken in New York today.

Ancient Rome
was eight times more
densely populated than
modern New York.

At the end of Roman mime plays,
audiences could demand that
the female lead strip on stage.

In the 1970s,
the British stripper Frank Jakeman
insured his penis for £1 million.

In Norway,
stripping counts as an art form
for tax purposes.

In the USA,
ransom payments to kidnappers
are tax-deductible.

In Armenia,
chess is a compulsory
school subject.

Eton College was founded
to provide free schooling
for poor boys.

Jean-Jacques Rousseau
gave all five of his children
to a foundling hospital
so they wouldn't interfere
with his work.

By the time they reach 17,
most British children
will have been driven
80,000 miles by their parents.

The average British child
makes its first mobile-phone call
at the age of eight.

There are 300,000
child soldiers
in the world.

There is only one pig in
Afghanistan.

Bush Market in Kabul,
named after George W. Bush,
sells food and supplies
stolen from US military bases.

When the British
invaded Afghanistan in 1839,
they brought 300 camel-loads of wine.

Camels have three sets of eyelids
and eight sets of eyelashes.

Dinosaurs
had no
eyelashes.

Crocodiles' faces
are ten times more sensitive
than human fingertips.

Alligators' penises
are permanently erect,
but concealed
inside their bodies.

Squirrels forget where they've buried
three-quarters of their nuts.

The most common place
to hide household valuables
is in the sock drawer;
this is also the first place
that burglars check.

Henrietta Maria,
wife of King Charles I,
pawned the Crown Jewels
to raise money for
the English Civil War.

Louis XIV had a coat with
123 diamond buttons on it.

Jacques Chirac,
president of France,
spent £60,000 a year on
spring vegetables.

The world's most expensive car,
a 1957 Ferrari Testarossa,
was sold in 2011
for £10,750,000.

The world's most expensive sheep
was sold in 2009
for £231,000.

A person who illegally exports sheep
is called an 'owler'.

Selling illegal cigarettes
is known by US police
as 'smurfing'.

The world's largest producer of cigarettes
is the Chinese government.

Urea, the main ingredient in urine,
is added to cigarettes
to enhance their flavour.

Tobacco companies
use kitty litter
to make cigars bigger.

US patent no. 3,234,948,
held by Stuart M. Stebbings,
is for cheese-flavoured cigarettes.

Feta is the
oldest-known cheese:
it is mentioned
in *The Odyssey*.

At the age of nine,
the Carthaginian leader Hannibal
took an oath of perpetual hatred
against the Romans.

At the age of ten,
Pharaoh Rameses II
was a captain in the army
and had his own harem.

The Roman emperor Caligula
took revenge on the sea
for sinking his father's fleet
by attacking the English Channel.

Kayak is an Inuit word meaning
'man's boat'; strictly speaking,
the Olympic women's version
should be called the *umiak* competition.

A bronze in kayaking
is Togo's only Olympic medal,
won in 2008 by a man who
had only been to Togo once.

There are only two
sets of escalators
in Wyoming.

Costa Rica is home
to the world's only
sloth orphanage.

A sloth can take a month
to digest a single meal.

Queen Victoria
could eat a seven-course meal
in under half an hour.

'Restaurants'
were originally meat soups
for 'restoring' strength.

When Menelik II,
emperor of Ethiopia,
felt unwell, he would eat
a few pages of the Bible.

The Bible is available in
2,426 languages.

More than 40%
of the world's Catholics
live in South America.

Pope John XII
was killed by a jealous husband
in the act of committing adultery.

Pope John XX
never existed.

Five of the last eight popes
died in years when
Wales won the
Six Nations rugby tournament.

In the Koran,
Jesus is mentioned
five times more often
than Mohammed.

Earthworms
have five hearts.

Only five in a thousand
seahorses
survive to adulthood.

Herbert Spencer,
who coined the phrase
'survival of the fittest',
was the only one of eight siblings
to reach adulthood.

Only 2%
of Kuwaitis
are over 65.

Centenarians
are the fastest-growing
demographic in the UK.

Henry Ford
could still do handstands
at the age of 75.

Basketball, racquetball, volleyball
and Father's Day
all began
in a YMCA.

More phone calls are made
on Mother's Day
than on any other day.

More reverse-charge calls
are made on Father's Day
than on any other day.

Male ants
do not
have fathers.

A queen ant
can fertilise her eggs
with sperm she's stored for 30 years.

A velvet ant
is a type of wasp.

Bees
are vegetarian wasps.

Bees turn nectar into honey
by regurgitating it into
the mouths of other bees.

The extinct gastric brooding frog
used her stomach as a womb
and gave birth by vomiting.

Woodchucks can't
'chuck-up'.

A tick is
ten times larger after dinner
than before.

Japanese yellow swallowtail butterflies
can see with their bottoms.

The potoo bird can see
with its eyes shut.

Chickens can see daylight
45 minutes before humans can.

Astronauts at the
International Space Station
witness 16 sunrises and sunsets
every 24 hours.

The pumping station
at Cricklewood
was used as the location
for the engine room
in the movie *Titanic*.

The first-ever
international cricket tour
had to be postponed due to
the French Revolution.

The first-ever
air-conditioning system
was installed in the
House of Commons.

The first-ever actress
to appear naked in a film
was called Louise Willy.

Sigmund Freud's
first research project
was on the sex life of the eel.

Eel blood
is toxic to humans.

The cigarette snail
is so called because
a bite from its venomous tooth
leaves you just enough time to
smoke a cigarette before you die.

Moths
can be trained to detect
plastic explosives.

Piranhas
enjoy beans and
other vegetables.

One in every 1,000
babies is born
with teeth.

The average age
of a human fat cell
is ten years.

Your eyebrows
renew themselves
every 64 days.

The human body
has the ability to regenerate
the tips of lost fingers or toes.

On Pluto, a 12-stone person
would weigh less than 12 pounds.

The atmospheric pressure
on Venus
is equivalent to being
half a mile under the sea
on Earth.

The volcanoes
on Jupiter's moon Io
spew fountains of lava
250 miles high.

Every winter
on Uranus
lasts for 42 years.

For Christmas 1936,
Salvador Dalí sent Harpo Marx
a harp with barbed-wire strings.
Harpo sent back a photograph
of himself with bandaged fingers.

Drachenfutter is
a present from a German to his wife
to apologise for being out late.
It means 'dragon fodder'.

In Canada,
Santa has his own postal code:
HOH OHO.

In 2009, a man dressed as Santa Claus
robbed a bank in Tennessee:
he claimed he needed money
to 'pay his elves'.

On any given day,
half of the world's population
are wearing jeans.

The small pocket
in the front of a pair of jeans
was designed for pocket watches.

In the 1840s,
trousers were known as
'sit-down-upons'.

The largest millipede
in Tanzania is known as
the wandering leg sausage.

Insects outnumber humans
by 200 million to one.

No more than two flies
are allowed by law
in any public toilet
in China.

The horse fly *Scaptia beyonceae*
is named for its
'pretty bootylicious'
golden abdomen.

A photo of Pamela Anderson
was taped to his handlebars
by cyclist Mario Cipollini
in the 1999 Tour de France
to boost his testosterone levels.

Wendy in *Peter Pan* was based on
the daughter of the man who inspired
Long John Silver in *Treasure Island*.

François le Clerc
is the only known pirate
to have had a peg-leg.

Sir Arthur Aston, Governor of Oxford
in the English Civil War,
was murdered in Ireland in 1649
by having his brains bashed out
with his own wooden leg.

In 1796, in a cricket match between
Greenwich Pensioners with One Arm and
Greenwich Pensioners with One Leg,
Greenwich Pensioners with One Leg
won by 103 runs.

Mark Twain said he wanted
to dig up Jane Austen and beat her
over the skull with her own shin bone.

If Jane Austen hadn't
broken off her engagement,
she would have been known as
Mrs Harris Bigg-Wither.

One in ten women
cares more for a fictional man
than for her partner.

Dame Judi Dench
has the James Bond theme
as her ringtone.

Almost everyone
living in Pompeii escaped
when Vesuvius erupted.

500 million people
are at risk from volcanoes
in the world today.

80% of the world's gold
was created by earthquakes.

Half the gold ever mined
has come from one place:
Witwatersrand, South Africa.

There is enough gold
in the Earth's core
to coat its entire surface
to a depth of 1.5 feet.

The amount of gold in
one human body is 0.2 mg;
to mint one gold sovereign
would need 40,000 people.

In the American Gold Rush,
only one in 25 prospectors
found any gold.

Using nuclear reactors,
it is possible to turn lead into gold;
though it is much easier
to turn gold into lead.

If North Dakota
were an independent nation,
it would be the world's
third-largest nuclear power.

Burning Mountain, Australia,
is a natural coal fire that has been
alight for 6,000 years.

Crayons, tights and aspirin
are all made from oil.

Russian bears
get high by sniffing
discarded aviation fuel.

Paddington Bear
was originally 'from darkest Africa'
until it was pointed out that
there are no bears in Africa.

50% of
people in India
do not have a lavatory.

40 million people
in China
live in caves.

Half the world's deaths
from air pollution
occur in China.

The Chinese state television company
is called CCTV.

Fortune cookies originated in America.
First imported to China in the 1990s,
they were advertised as
'Genuine American Fortune Cookies'.

The e-reader was invented
in 1949.

A group of kittens is called
a 'kindle'.

J. K. Rowling has no middle name.

Harry Potter in Calcutta (India),
Harry Potter and the Big Funnel (China)
and *Tanya Grotter and
the Magical Double Bass* (Russia)
are all Harry Potter rip-offs.

Working titles for
The Great Gatsby included
Trimalchio in West Egg and
The High-Bouncing Lover.

Something That Happened
was the original title of
John Steinbeck's
Of Mice and Men.

The first manuscript of
Of Mice and Men was chewed up
by John Steinbeck's dog, Toby.

A quarter of dog owners
sign their pet's name
on greeting cards.

A medium-sized tube of toothpaste
contains enough chemicals
to kill 13 dogs.

In the UK, you must legally report
a road accident involving a dog,
but not one involving a cat.

Wearing jeans is illegal
in North Korea.

Drink-driving is not illegal
in Indonesia.

Aborting a child because of its sex
is legal in Sweden.

Saudi Arabian women
are only allowed to ride bicycles
for 'entertainment purposes'.

In 1643, the Puritans
passed an act forbidding
'the ringing of bells for pleasure'.

The UK Shadow Business Secretary,
Chuka Umunna, was one of the choirboys
who sang the *Mr Bean* theme tune.

Until 1972,
the national anthem of the Maldives
was sung to the tune of
'Auld Lang Syne'.

In America,
Tarzan's yell
is a registered trademark.

In the 2009 *Star Trek* film,
Zachary Quinto could only
manage the Vulcan salute after
his fingers were glued together.

Two-thirds
of human communication
is by gesture,
not speech.

The Queen
does the washing-up once a year.
There's a special hut at Balmoral
for her to do it in.

78% of women say
they would love to receive
a romantic letter or poem,
but only 50% of men have ever
written either.

John Milton
sold the rights of *Paradise Lost*
for £10.

Arthur Conan Doyle
was one of the judges
at the world's first-ever
bodybuilding contest.

Stanley Kubrick
financed his early movies
by playing illegal chess for money
in New York parks.

The Spice Girls
are mentioned five times
in the *Oxford English Dictionary*,
under 'girl power', 'big',
'merchandised', 'popularist'
and 'tabloid'.

In the 19th century,
Goldilocks
was known as
Silver Hair.

In 19th-century versions of *Cinderella*,
her sisters called her 'Cinder-slut'.

Christian names in the Philippines
include Bing, Bong, Bambi, Bogie, Girlie,
Peanut and Bumbum.

President Aquino of the Philippines
is known as Noynoy
and his sisters are called
Pinky and Ballsy.

Wagner only ever wore
pink silk underwear.

After she died,
Queen Victoria's underwear
was divided up between her courtiers
and sold as souvenirs.

Tallulah Bankhead acted in *Lifeboat* (1944)
without any underpants on.
When the film crew complained,
the director Alfred Hitchcock said,
'I don't know whether that's a concern
for wardrobe or hairdressing.'

Johnny Depp collects Barbie dolls.

When Einstein saw his baby sister
for the first time, he thought she was a toy.
'Where are the wheels?' he asked.

Buzz Lightyear has more
space experience than Buzz Aldrin:
the toy spent 468 days there in 2008–9,
beating the record for the
longest human space flight.

Pixar devised the key characters
and plots of *A Bug's Life*, *WALL·E*,
Monsters Inc. and *Finding Nemo*
in a single lunch meeting.

In the average lunch,
you eat about 150,000
kilometres of DNA.

Before Norfolk's railway was built,
it was quicker to travel
to Amsterdam by sea
than to London by road.

In 2010, a traffic jam
near Beijing in China
stretched for 100 kilometres
and lasted nine days.

In any one week,
London Underground escalators
travel the equivalent of
twice round the world.

'Lunting'
is walking
at the same time as
pipe-smoking.

The Scots king
who succeeded Macbeth
was called Lulach the Idiot.

Denmark pawned the
Shetland Islands in 1468.
In theory, they could buy them back
for 60,000 florins.

In *Braveheart*,
Mel Gibson's
modern black jockey shorts
can be seen under his kilt.

Harris tweed is not made
on the Isle of Harris;
it's made on the
Isle of Lewis.

Sporrans
are traditionally made
from otters.

Sea otters have as many hairs
on each square centimetre
of their bodies
as human beings have
on their entire heads.

Fake soy sauce
can be made from
human hair.

Queen bumblebees
go bald
in old age.

Only one woman's age
is given in the Bible:
Abraham's wife, Sarah (127).

Old people who completed
secondary education as children
are, on average, a centimetre taller
than those who don't.

Half the brain
of an eight-year-old child
can be removed
with no ill effects.

Since the first stone tools were made,
the human brain
has tripled in size.

[161]

Your brain makes
a million new connections
every second.

Your brain uses
less power than
the light in your fridge.

Eigengrau ('brain grey')
is the colour your eyes see
in total darkness.

Elvis wore
blue suede shoes
to his senior prom.

Stephen Stills, Glen Campbell and
Charles Manson all failed their
auditions for The Monkees.

Chopin
only performed 30 concerts
in his entire life.

Irving Berlin
couldn't read or write music
and could only play the piano in F sharp.

When Beethoven conducted the premiere
of his Ninth Symphony in Vienna,
he was completely deaf.
After it ended, one of the soloists
had to turn him around
so he could see the audience applauding.

Public applause is
banned in Belarus.

In the 16th century,
French actors hired
rieurs (laughers) and
chatouilleurs (ticklers)
to sit in the audience
and cheer everyone up.

The sound of arguments
can affect the brains
of sleeping babies.

Gilbert and Sullivan
split up after an argument
about the cost of a carpet
at the Savoy Theatre.

There's a carpet shop
in Dublin called
'Lino Ritchie'.

Cardiff has a
tiling-supplies outlet called
'Bonny Tiler'.

Bristol has a
mobile kebab truck called
'Jason Donervan'.

Portsmouth has a
locksmith called
'Surelock Homes'.

In the Sherlock Holmes stories,
the first names of Moriarty
and his brother are
only mentioned once.
Both are called James.

James I of Scotland
was murdered in a sewer.

James II of Scotland
had a huge bright red birthmark,
which led to the nickname
'Fiery Face'.

James II of England
was known in Ireland as
'James the Be-Shitten'.

'Science' and 'shit' both come
from the ancient word *skheid*,
meaning to 'separate' or 'divide'.

Science students who
wear white lab coats
perform better in tests.

Ernest Rutherford, who said,
'All science is either physics
or stamp collecting,'
won the Nobel Prize for Chemistry.

The chemical company Bayer
lost the trademark for aspirin
as part of Germany's reparations for
the First World War.

Suicide causes more deaths
than murder and war combined.

Suicide was a criminal offence
in the UK until 1961.

Bacteria that catch viruses
may commit suicide to protect
their neighbours from infection.

The man who wrote
'I Do Like to Be Beside the Seaside'
killed himself after being
booed off stage in Glasgow.

All the property in Glasgow
is worth less than the houses in
Elmbridge, Surrey.

There are more people buried in
Brookwood cemetery in Surrey
than there are living in
Southampton, Swindon or Oldham.

Surrey libraries
account for one-fifth
of all UK borrowing of
E. L. James's *Fifty Shades of Grey*.

The *Kama Sutra*
provides advice on
tongue-twisters and cockfighting.

In the Middle Ages,
erect penises were thought to be
full of pressurised air.

The pistol shrimp
uses jets of water to generate
a sonic boom as loud as Concorde's.

'Skunk' comes
from the Algonquian word
seganku, meaning
'he who squirts'.

A startled hagfish
can unleash more than
five gallons of defensive slime.

Uliginous means
'having a slimy nature'.

Slugs dislike copper;
their slime reacts with it
and gives them an electric shock.

A slug's anus
is on its head.

A *shirime* is a
Japanese monster
with an eye
in place of an anus.

Buddy
Holly was
so short-sighted
he couldn't read the
top line of the eye chart.

Dante Gabriel Rossetti
always wore two
pairs of spectacles.

Schubert
slept with his glasses on,
in case he got an idea
during the night.

When he gets writer's block,
Dan Brown hangs upside down
to get his creative juices flowing.

A pipistrelle bat
weighs less than a 2p coin.

The copper in
a pre-1992 2p coin
is now worth
more than 3p.

In 2011, a Georgian woman,
digging for copper to sell as scrap,
sliced through a cable and cut off
the whole of Armenia from the Internet.

In 1999, the king of Bhutan
allowed his country Internet access
to celebrate his Silver Jubilee.

Thailand has a special language
used exclusively for
talking to the king.

Carl XVI of Sweden
is only the tenth Swedish king named Carl;
Carls I to VI were mythical.

Princess Lilian of Sweden
was born in Swansea,
the daughter
of a market trader.

Prince Philip
is 483rd in line
to the British throne.

Queen Elizabeth II is descended
from the Prophet Mohammed.

The Queen is
a Knight of the Elephant (Denmark),
a Knight of the Golden Fleece (Spain)
and a Knight of the White Eagle (Poland).

According to the 2011 census,
one in three Londoners
was born abroad.

Only 20% of the Royal Mint's coins
are made for the UK.

The first image
on American television
was the dollar sign.

China has a greater reserve
of US dollars than
the USA itself.

The ancient Chinese believed that
the thicker your earlobe,
the wealthier you would be.

The most expensive
coffee in the world is made from
the dung of Thai elephants.

The Anglo-Saxons
called the little finger the 'ear finger'
because it's the one you use
to pick wax out of your ears.

The Romans called
the middle finger
digitus impudicus,
the 'obscene' or 'offensive' finger.

Galileo's middle finger
is on display
at a museum in Florence.

Russian, Spanish and Persian
use the same words for
'fingers' as for 'toes'.

The fleshy bulb
at the base of your thumb
is called the *thenar*.

Elephants suck their trunks
as children suck their thumbs.

Rubik's cubers can
suffer from cubist's thumb
and Rubik's wrist.

The 'tiny arms' of
Tyrannosaurus rex
could each lift the equivalent of
two adult humans.

After losing his right arm in battle,
Horatio Nelson developed a
phantom limb in its place.
He considered it 'direct proof
for the existence of the soul'.

When three people
were rushed to hospital
in the 1990s with twisted intestines,
the Chinese state media issued
warnings about hula-hooping.

In the Dutch version of Cluedo,
Professor Plum is called
Professor Pimpel.

In the Polish version of Scrabble,
the letter Z is only worth
one point.

Znuz is an old word
for 'frost'.

Snowbroth is snow
which has been trodden
down into a mush.

New York gets
15 times as much snow
as the South Pole.

The snow on Venus
is made from heavy metals.

Until 323 BC,
Venus's appearances
in the morning and evening
were thought to be different planets.

Venus is the most common
natural object to be
mistaken for a UFO.

The most popular item
in the FBI's online reading room
is an unconfirmed report
of a UFO over New Mexico.

Abraham Lincoln
created the Secret Service
on the day he was shot.

Richard Nixon
applied unsuccessfully
to join the FBI.

The US Republican Party
hasn't won a presidential election
without a Bush or a Nixon on the ticket
since 1928.

The Democrats and Republicans
ran over a million TV ads in 2012:
it would take more than a year
to watch them all.

When George Washington campaigned
for election in Virginia in 1758,
he bought every eligible voter
three pints of alcohol.

Ebriety
is the opposite of
sobriety.

In the late Middle Ages,
you could pay taxes
with beer.

In 1695, the American colonies
levied a tax on bachelors
to encourage men to marry.

In 1831, only 3%
of the population of Britain
was eligible to vote.

Switzerland
only gave women the vote
in 1971.

The man who sent
the world's first email in 1971
can't remember what it said.

In 1973, British Rail
was granted a patent
for a spaceship.

The guillotine
was last used in France
in 1977.

The hollow bit in the top of a brick
is called a *frog*.

The wire cage holding the cork
in a bottle of champagne
is called an *agraffe*.

The metal clip for a light bulb
inside a lamp shade
is called a *harp*.

The head of a cauliflower
is called a *curd*.

The fermented-cabbage museum in Seoul
has 100,000 visitors a year.

South Korea has a toilet theme park
started by a Mr Duck,
who was born in
an outside lavatory.

There are 34,000 statues
of Kim Il Sung in North Korea.

90% of archaeological artefacts
in the UK are found by
amateur treasure hunters.

Only one pirate is known
to have buried
any treasure.

There is only one
recorded case
of 'walking the plank'.

There is no historical evidence
for any pirate having ever
owned a pet parrot.

Mrs Beeton's Book of Household Management
contains recipes for parrot pie,
roast wallaby and curried kangaroo.

Colonel Sanders' secret recipe
for Kentucky Fried Chicken
is written in pencil on a scrap of paper
and kept in a high-security vault
in Lexington, Kentucky.

The ingredient that
makes Brussels sprouts bitter
is cyanide.

15 apricot kernels
contain enough cyanide
to kill a child.

A key ingredient of gunpowder
is human urine.

Lobsters' bladders
are in their
heads.

The Chinese soft-shelled turtle
urinates through its
mouth.

The Vietnamese fish
Phallostethus cuulong
has its penis under its chin.

In 1994,
'Rasputin's severed penis'
was offered to an auction house,
but it turned out to be a
dried sea cucumber.

A sea cucumber eats
through its anus.

Slender pearlfish
live inside the bottoms
of sea cucumbers.

Cucumbers are 95% water.

All the instruments of the
First Vienna Vegetable Orchestra
are made into soup
after each performance.

John Cage's composition
0′0″ (1962) is for
chopped vegetables
and blender.

In 1941, Henry Ford
made a car
out of soy beans.

The man who built
the town stocks in Boston
charged so much he became
the first man to be punished in them.

Special Brew
was created by Carlsberg
in honour of Winston Churchill.

There is a brewer in Oregon
who makes beer from yeast
collected from his own beard.

According to Guinness,
162,719 pints of 'black gold'
are absorbed by beards
and moustaches each year.

Frank Beard
is the only member
of ZZ Top
who doesn't have a beard.

During the Napoleonic wars,
British troops referred to
French soldiers' moustaches as
'appurtenances of terror'.

Grenade
is French for
'pomegranate'.

Serviette
is French for
'briefcase'.

Motdièse
(or 'sharp-sign word')
was coined by the French in 2013
to avoid using the English word
'hashtag'.

Until 2013,
French had no word for French kissing.
Galocher ('to kiss with tongues')
is now an official entry in the 2014
Petit Robert French dictionary.

King John I of France
was proclaimed king
five months before he was born.
He only lived for five days.

Marie Thérèse, daughter of
Louis XVI and Marie Antoinette,
was queen of France
for 20 minutes.

A 'moment'
is officially defined as
90 seconds.

The average US shareholding
lasts 22 seconds.

The Mayan calendar
had five days a year
that were known as
'days with no name'.

The Saxon word for January
was *Wulfmonath*: the month
when starving wolves were
bold enough to enter villages.

In 15th-century France,
one in every four days was
an official holiday.

The Russian Olympic team
arrived 12 days late for the
1908 London Olympics because
they were still using the Julian Calendar.

The Royal Train
is never more than 15 seconds late
and must stop within six inches of its mark
or it will miss the red carpet.

All the departure boards at
Grand Central Station are
exactly one minute wrong.

All telephone services in the USA
were suspended for one minute
during the funeral of
Alexander Graham Bell.

The first mobile-phone call
took place on 3rd April 1973.
Motorola's general manager
called their rivals AT&T
to let them know they'd got there first.

Lord Byron was the first man to swim
from Europe to Asia.

John Maynard Keynes's mother, Florence,
was the first female mayor
of Cambridge.

The first-ever football chant
was written by
Edward Elgar.

Enid Blyton
liked to play tennis
in the nude.

The Famous Five never had
'lashings of ginger beer',
but they did have
'lashings of hard-boiled eggs'
and 'lashings of poisonous snakes'.

In Ian Fleming's original books,
James Bond drinks 101 whiskies
but only 19 vodka Martinis.

Roget's Thesaurus
has an index which is longer
than the book itself.

The most common book
people lie about having read is
George Orwell's *Nineteen Eighty-Four*.

George Orwell's French teacher
was Aldous Huxley.

Handel and Jimi Hendrix lived at
the same house in London
250 years apart.

Mozart once proposed to
Marie Antoinette.

Newborn babies like
Mozart and Vivaldi,
but are indifferent to Beethoven.

Beethoven
had particularly hairy hands.

Hairy-legged tights are sold in China
to protect girls from
unwanted male attention.

In ancient China,
panda fur
was used for
sanitary towels.

All the pandas in the world
belong to China.

30,000 dogs a day
are slaughtered in China
for meat and fur.

The Swiss
are the only Europeans
who eat dog meat.

There are enough
nuclear shelters in Switzerland
to house the entire population.

66% of Mumbai's inhabitants
live in just 8%
of the city's area.

36,000 people in Bangladesh
talk Koch.

The British surname 'Cock'
is four times less common today
than it was in 1881.

The most popular name in China is Wang:
there are 93 million Wangs in China.

Welshite
is a mineral named after its discoverer,
Wilfred R. Welsh.

In Indonesian,
a *jayus* is a joke
so terrible and badly told
that it becomes funny.

Until the mid-19th century,
Indonesia's Banda Islands
were the world's only source
of nutmeg and mace.

Chemical Mace,
the protective spray,
is named after the medieval weapon
not the spice.

Salt and pepper are
provided by NASA for astronauts
in liquid form.

Silly Putty
was taken on Apollo 8
to secure tools in
weightless conditions.

It is impossible
to whistle in a
spacesuit.

Dolphins use
their unique whistles
to call each other
by 'name'.

Ne Win,
former prime minister of Burma,
bathed in dolphin's blood,
believing it kept him
youthful.

Dolphins
can stay awake
for 15 days at a time.

Sloths
sleep for ten hours in the wild,
but 16 hours in zoos.

People who
suffer from *dysania*
find it difficult to
get out of bed in the morning.

Tragomaschalia is
having smelly armpits.

Human body odour
is irresistible to
female goats
on heat.

The South American *hoatzin*
or 'stink bird' has the
slowest digestion of any bird and
smells strongly of rotting manure.

The best way to repel a shark
is to wave rotting flesh
from one of its dead relatives at it.

A single rotten log in a forest
contains between 300 and 400
species of fungi.

Kiwis smell like
field mushrooms.

Franz Schubert was short and fat.
His friends called him 'the mushroom'.

Schubert was a pall-bearer
at Mozart's funeral.

William Walton
became a composer
'to get away from Oldham'.

The explorer Thor Heyerdahl
once spent hours waiting for a taxi
at the BBC only to find that
the driver had been there all along,
waiting for 'four Airedales'.

The first woman to run
the 400-metre hurdles
in under 53 seconds
was called
Marina Stepanova.

In 2012, the Olympic hurdler
Vania Stombolova
failed to reach the semi-finals
after she fell at the first hurdle.

In February 2013, Hartlepool United
beat Notts County 2–1. Hartlepool's
scorers were Hartley and Poole.

In a 90-minute football match,
the average player is
in possession of the ball
for 53.4 seconds.

The only football team
with a 100% win rate against Barcelona
is Dundee United.

Manchester United FC
started out as Newton Heath LYR
(Lancashire and Yorkshire Railway) FC.

The first professional baseball team
was the Cincinnati Red Stockings.

Before forming The Beatles,
Lennon and McCartney
billed themselves as
The Nerk Twins.

Simon and Garfunkel
were originally called
Tom and Jerry.

Tom and Jerry
were originally called
Jasper and Jinx.

New Jersey
was originally called
Lorraine.

Oxford Circus and Piccadilly Circus
were both once called Regent Circus.
The present names were invented by
bus drivers to avoid confusion.

Bus Company Island
is a nature reserve
in Kent.

Nottingham
was first named Snottingham,
after a Viking called Snot.

Names of British castles include
Almond, Cadbury, Cooling,
Eye, Fail, Fast and Stalker.

There are towns in Kentucky called
Twenty-six, Seventy-six
and Eighty-eight.

The four highest mountains on Earth,
Everest, K2, Kanchenjunga and Lhotse,
were first scaled in
1953, 1954, 1955 and 1956
respectively.

As well as K2,
there are four other mountains
too remote to have local names:
K7, K9, K12 and K25.

The world's highest unclimbed peak
is Gangkhar Puensu in Bhutan.
The mountain is considered sacred
and climbing above 6,000 metres
is banned by the government.

According to Mormonism,
the Garden of Eden
was in Missouri.

A *gobemouche* is someone who
believes anything
they're told.

'DOH'
is the abbreviation for
Doha International Airport
in Qatar.

Saudi Arabia
imports sand.

In the ancient Kush Empire
of North Africa,
a double chin was considered
the height of beauty.

The point of the chin
is called
the *pogonion.*

Bed makers Silent Night
employ a professional bed tester
whose bottom is insured
for £1 million.

William Pitt the Younger
was so thin he was nicknamed
'The Bottomless Pitt'.

After pregnancy,
women have permanently
larger feet.

The lower the ratio between
a man's index and ring fingers,
the longer his penis will be.

Some sea slugs
use a new penis
every time they have sex.

A 'School of Undressing' was founded
for women in Manhattan in 1937,
in the belief that
'poor disrobing techniques'
were driving up divorce rates.

The Yagan of Australia
use *mamihlapinatapei* to mean
'the wordless yet meaningful look
shared by two people who desire
to initiate something, but who
are both reluctant to start'.

The Amondawa people
of the Amazon
have no word for 'time'.

Latin and Gaelic have no words
for 'yes' or 'no'.

Sgiomlaireachd (pron. scum-leerie)
is a Scots Gaelic word meaning
'the kind of friend who
only drops in at
mealtimes'.

To *groak* is to silently watch
people while they're eating,
hoping they'll ask you to join them.

Twice as many forks as knives
are sold in the UK:
Britons increasingly
eat with just a fork.

To *pingle* is a
Norfolk word meaning
to play with your food.

The makers of Pringles
won a court case in 2008
arguing that Pringles aren't crisps.
The verdict was overturned
the following year.

People are 50% heavier
and four inches taller
than they were in 1900;
the biggest changes to the
human body for 50 centuries.

Brazils, cashews, coconuts,
peanuts and walnuts
are not nuts.

Juglandaceous
means
'walnutty'.

One jar of Nutella
is sold somewhere in the world
every 2.5 seconds.

In 2011, a lorry crashed on the M1
spilling enough Marmite
to cover 24 million slices of toast.

Until rubber's uses were discovered
in 1770, pencil marks were erased
using lumps of fresh bread.

The best thing before sliced bread
was wrapped bread.
Sliced bread was advertised as
'The Greatest Forward Step
Since Bread Was Wrapped'.

Ciabatta bread
was invented in 1982.

Baker's yeast and humans
share 18% of their genes.

To read someone's
entire genome out loud
would take nine and a half years.

In a single day,
a cow produces
up to 320 pints
of saliva.

To *flink*
is to behave in
a cowardly manner.

Boanthropy is
the delusion that you are
an ox or cow.

Buffalo Bill
killed bison,
not buffalo.

The word 'snapshot'
was first used in 1808.
It meant 'to fire at a fast-moving
target without aiming properly'.

When taking snaps,
the French say *ouistiti* ('marmoset'),
the Bulgarians say *zele* ('cabbage'),
the Estonians say *hernesupp* ('pea soup')'
and the Thais say *pepsi*
instead of 'cheese'.

Over half the cheese
eaten in the UK
is Cheddar.

The ploughman's lunch
was invented in 1956 by the
English Country Cheese Council.

Until the 15th century, 'cake' meant
a flat, round loaf of bread.

Before cane sugar
was introduced to Europe,
food was often sweetened
with parsnips.

As the Earth moves
it makes a musical note
too low for human hearing:
C sharp, 29 octaves below middle C.

Nobody has ever lasted
more than 45 minutes
in the world's quietest room.

In its entire lifespan,
the average home power drill
in the UK is only used
for 20 minutes.

Steering wheels weren't introduced
to British cars until 1898.
The first cars had steering tillers.

Killer whales
were originally called
'whale killers'.

Only one
person is
known to have
been killed by a centipede.

The black mamba is not black;
it gets its name from
the colour of the
inside of its mouth.

An old name for the kestrel is
windfucker.

Fox tossing
was a popular 17th-century sport;
the fox was fired into the air
using a sling.

Dubai's Burj Khalifa skyscraper
is so high, and its lifts are so fast,
that you can watch the sun set
at ground level, travel to the roof
and watch it set again.

The first skyscrapers
were buildings with ten to 20 floors;
today they are defined as
those with more than 40.

Locust swarms move so fast because
each locust is trying to eat the one in front
and avoid being eaten by the one behind.

Albatrosses
can fly around the world
in less than two months.

A Formula 1 racing car
could get round the M25
in 48 minutes.

Apollo 11's flag is
no longer standing on the Moon.
It was planted too close to the
lunar module's lift-off site
and was blown over
by the exhaust.

Exhaust emissions
can be reduced
by using pig's urine.

22 of the first 29
US astronauts
were firstborns.

More people have
been into space
than have seen
a snow tiger in the wild.

Snow leopards
used to be called
'ounces'.

Astatine
is an element so rare
there is only an ounce of it
in the whole world.

More chemical elements
have been discovered in Britain
than in any other country.

Over 98% of
the Earth's crust
is made of only eight
chemical elements.

Half the mass
of most rock
is oxygen.

One gram of matter
contains as much energy
as 10,000 tonnes of TNT.

The mass of a Higgs boson is
0.000000000000000000000003 grams.

CERN is home to
the world's largest magnet:
it weighs more than
the Eiffel Tower.

The paint on the Eiffel Tower
weighs as much as
ten elephants.

The water melting
from the Greenland ice sheet
each year weighs as much as
a hundred million bowhead whales
or a billion elephants.

The polar ice cap is melting
so quickly that, by 2050,
ships will be able to sail
to the North Pole.

If the temperature
in the UK reaches 50°C,
the roads will melt.

The Earth's core
is about the same temperature
as the surface of the sun.

In 1673, Dover and Calais
were joined by ice.

There are more deer
in Britain today
than at any time
since the last Ice Age.

Fighting male deer
can lock antlers
and starve to death.

Moose masturbate
by rubbing their
antlers on trees.

Egyptian pharaohs
ritually masturbated into the Nile
to ensure an abundance of water.

Rose water was the
world's most popular flavour
until the discovery of vanilla.

The technical term
for ice-cream brain freeze is
sphenopalatine ganglioneuralgia.

Japanese ice-cream flavours include:
cactus, raw horseflesh,
squid gut, pit viper, goat,
charcoal, collagen and Viagra.

In the 12th century,
one in ten Japanese
was a Samurai.

In 1602, the Japanese government
ordered all pet cats be released
to kill the mice threatening
the country's silkworms.

In the Pyrenees
in the 18th century,
farmers buried live cats
to clear their land of weeds.

The magic word
'abracadabra'
was first used to
ward off malaria.

There is a cult in Malaysia
that worships
a giant teapot.

The philosopher Jeremy Bentham
had a special teapot called Dickey.

In Tibet,
distances were traditionally measured
by the number of cups of tea
needed for each journey.

Britons drink
60 billion cups of tea
every year.

In 2011, under pressure from
animal-rights activists,
PG Tips agreed to stop testing
its tea on animals.

In the UK, octopuses enjoy
the same legal status as vertebrates.

An octopus has horizontal pupils;
whatever angle the octopus is at,
its pupils always stay aligned
with the horizon.

There is a fish
that mimics an octopus
mimicking a fish.

Prozac makes fish angry.

80% of front-page newspaper articles
are written by men.

More Nobel Peace Prizes
have been awarded to institutions
than to women.

Only 5% of the art
currently on display
in American museums
is by women.

The average woman spends
16 months of her life
crying.

Saudi Arabia has
the highest motor accident rate
in the world
and no women drivers.

Three times as many
Japanese people die
in bathtubs as in car crashes.

88% of adult Italians
have had sex in a car.

Tormentone is the Italian for
a summer hit song that is always
playing on your car radio.

Fiat is an acronym of
the Italian for
'Italian Car Factory of Turin'.

BMW stands for
the German for
'Bavarian Motor Works'.

Mazda is the ancient
Zoroastrian god of wisdom.

Samsung
means 'three stars'
in Korean.

Mitsubishi means
'three water chestnuts'
in Japanese.

CT body scans expose the patient
to the same amount of radiation
as that experienced within a mile
and a half of the Hiroshima bomb.

Marie Curie exposed herself
to so much radiation
that her kitchen cookbooks
are still radioactive.

In 1930, a radium-infused jockstrap
called the Scrotal Radiendocrinator
went on the market,
claiming to boost sexual virility.

A *spermologer*
is a collector of trivia.

Koinophilia
is sexual attraction to
average people.

Economics students
have more sexual partners
than those of any other subject.

Semen and *seminar*
both come from
the Latin for
'seed' or 'offspring'.

The mean cost of
bringing up a British child
is estimated to be
£218,024.

Regular use of sunblock has
increased the incidence of rickets
among British children.

American children get
11% of their daily energy intake
from sugary drinks.

By 2050, one in three Americans
will be diabetic.

During the
Seven Years War (1754–63),
1,512 British soldiers were killed in action
and 100,000 were killed by scurvy.

In 1915, more men died
on the Western Front
than the total number of yards
gained by either side.

80% of men born
in the Soviet Union in 1923
were dead by 1945.

China's Taipang Rebellion (1850–64)
killed 20 million people:
a tenth of the world's population.

The first country to ban *foie gras*
on grounds of animal cruelty
was Nazi Germany.

Of almost 4,000 mammals
in Berlin Zoo in 1939,
only 91 survived the bombings
of the Second World War.

Half the world's 6,000 languages
are not expected to survive
into the next century.

An *apocaholic* is a person
obsessed with the possibility
of imminent disaster.

.

Human settlement in the Pacific islands
has led to the disappearance
of a tenth of the world's
bird species.

Animals found only in Fiji
include the montane emo skink,
the bicolored foxface and the
twilight fangblenny.

In Fiji, until 2003,
Prince Charles's birthday
was a national holiday.

Hawaii is the only US state
that still has the Union Jack
as part of its flag.

The largest ship ever built
was too big to sail through
the English Channel.

Venice's Grand Canal isn't a canal,
it's a seawater channel.

'Bach' means brook or stream.
Beethoven once remarked that Bach
should be known as 'ocean',
not 'brook'.

At its mouth,
the Amazon River is nearly as wide
as the Thames is long.

A raindrop that falls
into the Thames will pass
through the bodies of eight people
before it reaches the sea.

It is impossible
to suck water up through a straw
more than 34 feet long.

Fell Beck Falls in Yorkshire
is twice the height of Niagara.

The second-highest waterfall in Canada
doesn't have a name.

Toronto has a
sports accessories store named
'The Merchant of Tennis'.

Canada's Olympic lacrosse team of 1904
had players called Rain-in-Face,
Snake Eater and Man Afraid Soap.

Writer Ambrose Bierce's siblings
were Abigail, Amelia, Ann, Addison,
Aurelius, Augustus, Almeda, Andrew,
Albert, Arthur, Adelia and Aurelia.

Annabelle, Daisy, Emma, Elizabeth,
Gabriel, Joshua, Lulu, Maxine, Nicola,
Sebastian, Vanessa, Verity and Winston
are all varieties of potato.

[247]

Dutch poets you may not know include
Jacob Cats, Hans Plomp, Hubert Poot,
Wieny Curvers and Antony Staring.

Cristiano Ronaldo's full name is
Cristiano Ronaldo dos Santos Aveiro.
He was named after
Ronald Reagan.

Ronald Reagan's
chief of staff was called
Donald Regan.

The General Secretary
of the Sri Lanka Teachers' Union
is called Joseph Stalin.

There is a peer in the House of Lords
called Lady Garden.

Between 2002 and 2010,
335 people visited A&E in America
with pubic-hair-grooming injuries.

New Yorkers
bite 25 times more Americans
than sharks do.

A 1998 health-and-safety report
in Queensland, Australia,
advised against placing
'any part of one's body
in the mouth of a crocodile'.

In Queensland,
pet rabbits are illegal.

In Melbourne,
singing an obscene ballad is
punishable by six months in prison.

The name Canberra
resulted from a competition;
losing entries included
Democratia, Kangaremu
and Australamooloo.

When people first came to
Australia 40,000 years ago,
the land was covered with
tropical forests, brimming lakes
and snow-capped mountains.

A 2013 survey found
that 10% of Britons think
that Australia is further away
than the Moon.

The inflexible gloves that
astronauts wear cause
their fingernails to fall off.

The only mountain in Flanders
is 156 metres high.

First prize at the 2010
Karaoke World Championships
in Moscow was
one million dumplings.

The doomed *Hindenburg* airship was
equipped with a cigarette lighter;
it was chained to a table
in the smoking room.

'Flak' is an abbreviation
of the German word
Fliegerabwehrkanone
'pilot warding-off cannon'.

A *temherte slaq* is an
Ethiopian punctuation mark
used to denote sarcasm.

In Finnish
an exclamation mark
is a 'shout mark';
in Spanish it's
a 'wonder symbol'.

Ruyton-XI-Towns, Shropshire,
is the only place in Britain
whose name contains Roman numerals.

In Roman law, *balnearii* were
criminals who stole
clothes from public baths.

The Roman army
used cobwebs
to dress wounds.

Spiders recycle their webs
by eating them.

Black-lace weaver spiders
increase their chances of survival
by eating their mother
before leaving the nest.

The average Briton
thinks there are
25 times as many
teenage mothers
as there actually are.

Osburgh, first wife of Ethelwulf,
was the mother of four English kings:
Ethelbald, Ethelbert, Ethelred I
and Alfred the Great.

Karl Marx's mother once said to him:
'I wish you would make some capital
instead of just writing about it.'

A new law in China in 2013
means citizens could face jail
if they don't visit their parents.

The average British woman
owns 22 items of clothing
that she never wears.

For 214 years until 2012,
it was illegal in Paris
for women to wear trousers.

Women's size 14 trousers
are four inches bigger
at the waist today
than they were in the 1970s.

Robert Wadlow,
the tallest man in history,
went to school at the age of five
in a suit made for a 17-year-old.

Straitjackets used to be known
as 'strait-waistcoats'.

The first piece of
high-visibility clothing
was a wedding dress.

The first heart pacemaker
had a battery that was
wheeled around in a cart.

In 1961, a Soviet surgeon
in Antarctica became
the first person to successfully
remove his own appendix.

In 1974,
the Soviet Union
drew up detailed plans
to invade Manchester.

Russia's legal minimum
monthly wage is £93.
The minimum monthly
cost of living there is £125.

Knowing that Angela Merkel
is afraid of dogs, Vladimir Putin
arrived to meet her in 2007
with his black Labrador.

The word 'bully'
once meant
'sweetheart'.

The man who voiced
Mickey Mouse
for 32 years
married the woman
who voiced Minnie Mouse
for 27 years.

The actors who play Homer and Marge
in the French version of *The Simpsons*
are married in real life.

The married actors who voiced
Popeye and Olive Oyl
ate spinach at their wedding.

Paul Winchell, the man who voiced
Wacky Races villain Dick Dastardly,
built and patented the
first artificial heart in 1956.

Mel Blanc, the voice of Bugs Bunny,
has 'That's All Folks!'
inscribed on his tombstone.

A whole series of *The Flintstones*
was recorded in Mel Blanc's bedroom
when he was in a full-body cast
after a car accident.

Walt Disney
was so poor in his twenties,
he had to eat dog food.

Frederick the Great of Prussia
drank coffee mixed with
champagne and mustard.

Charles II massaged his body with
dust from mummified pharaohs
in the hope that their 'greatness'
would rub off on him.

John Major failed
the selection process
to become a
bus conductor.

The first woman to run a
post office in Germany was
later burned as a witch.

The average keyboard
contains 3,295 germs
per square inch.

The first computer mouse
was called an
x–y position indicator.

At any given second,
6 million space bars are being hit
around the world.

When the *Mona Lisa* was stolen
from the Louvre in 1911,
people flocked to look at
the space where it had been.

'Extramundane'
describes the empty space
in which the universe sits.

The silent letters
in words like 'knife' are called
aphthongs.

Bodhidharma,
the founder of Zen Buddhism,
spent nine years sitting
facing a wall.

From 1814 to 1830,
the French flag was
plain white.

Brown dwarf stars
are red or blue,
but never
brown.

Dung beetles
navigate using
the Milky Way.

The largest known black holes
are 20 billion times
more massive than the Sun.

39 digits of pi are enough to measure
the circumference of the universe
to the accuracy of the width of
a hydrogen atom.

The atom-bomb explosion at Hiroshima
was generated by matter weighing
no more than a paper clip.

The weight of the cows in any field
will always be less than
the weight of the worms beneath it.

When he died, Dr Atkins
(of the best-selling Atkins diet)
weighed over 18 stones.

Ben & Jerry became friends
at gym class after the coach
shouted at them for being
'the two slowest, fattest kids'.

Obesity
kills three times as many people
as malnutrition.

One-third of Americans
have eaten cold pizza
for breakfast.

Cornflakes
have more salt per ounce
than salted peanuts.

There's only a one-calorie difference
between a bowl of Frosties
and a bowl of Special K.
(The extra calorie is in Special K.)

Following Hurricane Katrina,
the use of names beginning with K
increased by 9%.

There are only four people called Kevin
in the *Dictionary of National Biography*,
and one of them is a woman.

In 1880, 46 baby girls born in the USA
were given the name John, 14 were
named Cecil and 13 were called Frank.

St Kevin is
the patron saint of blackbirds.

In the first quarter of 2012,
Apple sold more iPhones than
there were babies born in the world.

Londoners check their phones
150 times a day,
or once every six minutes.

The average UK office worker
gets 40 emails a day and almost half
never post a letter.

One in four British relationships
begin online.

One in every seven
minutes spent online is
spent on Facebook.

Six new articles
are published on Wikipedia
every second.

The word 'twitter' was first used
by Geoffrey Chaucer
in 1374.

The average Briton will text
the equivalent of two copies of
the *Complete Works of Shakespeare*
in a lifetime.

William Shakespeare
is an anagram of
'I am a weakish speller'.

The scientific name for kookaburras,
Dacelo, is an anagram of *Alcedo*,
the scientific name for kingfishers.

Monday is the only day of the week
with a single-word anagram ('dynamo').

Cornish Yarg cheese
was invented by the Gray family;
Yarg is 'Gray' spelt backwards.

The fax machine was invented
30 years before the telephone.

The remote control
was developed during
the First World War
by the German army.

In the First World War,
it was patriotic in the UK
to kick dachshunds.

In the Second World War,
the Americans renamed
German measles
'liberty measles'.

The cougar, or mountain lion,
holds the Guinness World Record
for the animal with the most names:
it has more than 40 in English alone.

The South American bullfrog
is eaten as a delicacy in Dominica,
where it is known as
'mountain chicken'.

The mountain goat is not a goat,
the mountain ash is not an ash
and mountain spinach is not spinach.

The 'naked mole rat'
is neither naked, a mole
nor a rat.

The circus performer Pasqual Pinon
was known as the 'Two-headed Mexican'.
He only had one head
and came from Texas.

Seven Mile Beach
on Grand Cayman is
five and a half miles long.

The town of Sevenoaks
is home to eight oaks.

Tuvalu means
'cluster of eight' in Tuvaluan.
There are nine islands
in Tuvalu.

The Royal Train
is nine carriages long.

The Andorran army
is made up of ten soldiers.

You can fold a piece of paper
in half 13 times.

Bolivia
has 37 official languages.

Laotian rock rats were
thought to be extinct for 11 million years
until one was found for sale
in a market in Laos in 2006,
about to be turned into a kebab.

One in five doner kebabs
in the UK poses a 'significant'
threat to public health.

The average British kebab
contains 98% of a person's
daily salt requirement.

Penguins
can drink salt water.

Captain Scott's
expedition to the South Pole
ate stewed penguin for
Christmas dinner.

Charles Darwin once ate
roast armadillo
and said he preferred it to duck.

Darwin's tortoise Harriet
died in 2006
at the age of 176.

The dinosaur noises in *Jurassic Park*
were made using recordings
of tortoises having sex.

Moths can confuse bats' ultrasound
by wiggling their genitals.

Whales navigate hundreds of miles
using a mental map created by
bouncing sound off the sea floor.

There are more than 3 million
shipwrecks under the world's oceans.

Even when adjusted for inflation,
the movie *Titanic* cost
50% more to make than
the ship of the same name.

94% of the world's information
is stored digitally.

90% of all the data
ever produced by humans
was created in the last two years.

Every two days,
Facebook records more 'likes'
than there are people in the world.

The Internet domain name
Googlesucks.com
is owned by
Google.

IBM was originally called the
Computing-Tabulating-Recording
Company.

The first computer mouse
was made of wood.

The first golf balls
were made of wood.

The first golf tees
were little piles of sand.

Every grain of sand
on the planet
is unique.

Deserts make up 33%
of the Earth's surface,
but only 20% of them
are sandy.

The world's sandiest desert
is the Great Sandy in Australia,
but even that is only 50% sand.

Foster's,
the Australian beer company,
is the world's second-biggest
producer of wine.

Americans were so certain
crime was caused by alcohol
that, on the eve of Prohibition,
some towns in Iowa sold their jails.

A bank robbery
that takes place out of office hours
is classed as a mere burglary.

In 2013, a Milan court sentenced
a homeless man to house arrest.
Each night, police went round to his
bit of pavement to make sure
he was in his sleeping bag.

Sir Thomas Malory,
author of *Le Morte d'Arthur*,
was the only person in England
who wasn't pardoned after
the Wars of the Roses.

Abraham Lincoln
was inducted into the
Wrestling Hall of Fame.

Before he became a writer,
Franz Kafka was an
accident insurance lawyer.

Oliver Cromwell was a
farmer until he was 40.

Al Capone's business card
described him as
a used-furniture dealer.

In 1980,
Saddam Hussein
was awarded the key
to the city of Detroit.

Mussolini's son
was a top jazz musician.

Fidel Castro's son
is a champion golfer.

General Franco
kept the mummified hand of
St Teresa of Avila
on his bedside table
until his death.

American novelist
Sherwood Anderson
died from swallowing
the toothpick in the olive
in his Martini.

Dostoevsky's father
was drowned in vodka
by his own serfs.

Rodin died of pneumonia
brought on by cold
after being refused a room
in the centrally heated museum
where his sculptures were kept.

Eugene Aserinsky,
one of the founders of sleep research,
died in a car crash
after falling asleep at the wheel.

Everyone sleeps
in one of six different positions:
'foetus', 'log', 'yearner',
'soldier', 'freefaller'
or 'starfish'.

The technical term
for sleep-talking is
somniloquy.

Most people dream
five times a night.

The 'mare' in 'nightmare'
was a female demon
who suffocated people in their sleep
by sitting on their chests.

Cocaine, LSD, speed and crystal meth
are not narcotics.

Ernest Shackleton took cocaine
with him to the Antarctic
to combat snow blindness.

Pope Leo XIII carried
a hip flask full of wine
infused with cocaine.

Coca-Cola
started out as
the non-alcoholic version
of cocaine-based claret.

'Alcohol'
is from the Arabic *al-kuhl,*
meaning
'the essence of things'.

There is a cloud in
the constellation Aquila
that has enough alcohol in it to make
400 trillion trillion pints of beer.

The world's oldest legal system,
in ancient Mesopotamia,
established beer as a
unit of currency.

The punishment
for serving bad beer
in ancient Babylon
was drowning.

Robert Oppenheimer,
'the father of the atomic bomb',
tried to kill his university tutor
with a poisoned apple.

In the Second World War,
the USA and New Zealand
secretly tested 3,700 'tsunami bombs'
designed to destroy coastal cities.

In 1958, the US Air Force
lost a hydrogen bomb
somewhere in Georgia.

In 2012, a Mr Kaboom of Akron, Ohio,
caused panic after leaving
an aluminium walking stick
engraved with his surname
outside City Hall.

In 1916, Samuel Born
was given the key to
the city of San Francisco
for inventing the machine that
inserts sticks into lollipops.

The ancient Greek for 'little sticks'
is 'bacteria'.

The word 'mistletoe'
comes from the Anglo-Saxon for
'dung on a stick'.

When greeting one another,
white-faced capuchin monkeys
stick their fingers
up each other's noses.

King Alexander I of Greece
died after being bitten
by a pet monkey.

George IV
had a pet giraffe.

Henrik Ibsen
kept a pet scorpion
in an empty beer glass
on his desk.

Lord Kitchener
had four spaniels called
Shot, Bang, Miss
and Damn.

You only need to be
three feet underwater
to be protected from bullets.

The world record for
holding one's breath underwater
is 22 minutes.

Newborn rats
can survive underwater
for 40 minutes.

In the first century AD,
polar bears fought seals
in Roman amphitheatres
flooded with water.

Every year, hundreds of
elephant seal pups are crushed to death
under mating adults.

Elephant seal milk
is twice as thick as
whipping cream.

Baikal seals live in Lake Baikal,
2,500 miles from the sea.
Nobody knows how they got there.

Nobody knows
who invented the fire hydrant:
the patent records
were destroyed in a fire.

Ignivomousness
is the ability
to vomit fire.

In the 19th century,
angry cats were known as
'spitfires'.

The first Xerox photocopier
was so prone to bursting into flames
that it was fitted with its own
fire extinguisher.

The first cloned cat
was called 'CC',
short for
'Carbon Copy'.

Great white sharks
are 200 times heavier
than domestic cats,
but their brains
weigh almost the same.

A domestic cat
has a stronger bite
than a Komodo dragon.

Komodo dragons
eat up to 80% of their body weight
in a single meal.

Fleas can live for a year
without eating.

The UK's largest flea
lives on the pygmy shrew,
the UK's smallest mammal.

A colony of the world's smallest ants
could live comfortably inside the skull
of the world's largest ant.

The AD/BC dating system
was devised by a monk called
Dennis the Small.

Dennis, Kevin, Justin and Marvin
are the least likely names
to be clicked on by women
on dating websites.

The words 'whore' and 'charity'
both come from
a Germanic word meaning
'one who desires'.

George IV only had sex
with his wife, Caroline of Brunswick,
three times,
all in the first two days
of their marriage.

According to English folklore,
if a woman feeds her husband roast owl,
he will become completely subservient
to her every wish.

A male hippo
attracts a female by spraying her
with excrement.

A Mills and Boon-style romance
in France is called
a 'rose-water novel'.

In China, the Korean War is called
'The War to Resist US Aggression
and Aid Korea'.

The Japanese word *inemuri*
means 'sleeping on the job';
the practice is supposed to show
how committed an employee is.

A *hikikimori* is a
Japanese teenager who
spends most of their time
in their bedroom.

An *umbratile*
is someone who
stays in the dark.

US President Calvin Coolidge
liked to eat breakfast in bed
while having his head rubbed
with Vaseline.

Vaselina
is the Mexican title for
the movie
Grease.

Mexicans drink
more Coca-Cola per head
than anyone else.

Pope Benedict XVI drank
more than five times his own body weight
in Fanta every year.

The total amount of water
ever drunk by humans
would cover the Earth's oceans to
a depth of less than three millimetres.

Almost two-thirds
of all the water used in the UK
comes from other countries.

Only 22 of the
world's 193 countries
have never been invaded
by the British.

Americans
have invaded Canada twice,
in 1775 and 1812.
They lost both times.

2009
was the first year
in recorded history that there were
no executions in Europe.

2013 was the first year since 1987
composed of four different
digits.

1457 was the first year
the word 'golf'
appeared in print,
in an Act of Parliament
making it illegal.

The invention of the bicycle
increased the average distance between the
birthplaces of spouses in England
from one mile to 30 miles.

A human sperm
can swim 25 times its body length
every second.

If you laid all the viruses
in Earth's oceans end to end,
they would make a line
100 million light years long,
passing 50,000 galaxies.

Just looking at a sick person
is enough to get your
immune system
working.

Abraham Lincoln was suffering
from smallpox when he gave
the Gettysburg Address.

Alfred Russel Wallace was delirious
with a malarial fever
when he came up with
the Theory of Natural Selection.

The human influenza virus
was first isolated in 1933
from a sick ferret.

A flu virus
can only survive
on most surfaces for 48 hours,
but can live on a banknote
for 17 days.

The Bank of England
used to heat its buildings
by incinerating old banknotes.

La Paz, Bolivia,
was the first South American city
to get an electricity supply.
It was powered by llama dung.

Until 2010,
the solar-panel industry
used more electricity
than it produced.

You would need to cover an area
the size of Wales with wind turbines
to meet one-sixth of the UK's
daily energy needs.

One-third of batteries are thrown away
with 70% of their power left.

Sugar is an ingredient
in 70% of manufactured food.

70% of Americans
believe in angels.

In a 2004 experiment,
70% of Britons handed over
their computer passwords
in exchange for chocolate.

For 2,000 years,
chocolate was only known as a drink.
The first solid chocolate bar
was sold in 1849.

Hot chocolate seems tastier
if served in a cup
that is coloured
orange or cream.

Aristotle believed
rainbows only had
three colours.

To the Chinese,
rainbows have only
five colours.

You can only see a rainbow
if your back is to the sun.

A comet's tail always faces
away from the sun:
it doesn't tell you anything
about the way it's going.

You are ten times more likely
to be hit by a comet
than to die in a plane crash.

The word 'comet' is from the Greek
kometes meaning
'long-haired'.

Ponytails were
outlawed in China
in 1911.

In the 18th century,
to 'queue' meant
to tie your hair into a plait.

The French for 'grand piano'
— *piano à queue* —
means 'piano with a tail'.

Spotted animals
can have striped tails,
but stripy animals
can't have spotty tails.

Because they are
such solitary animals,
there is no collective noun
for a group of snow leopards.

Sami people
never mention a polar bear by name
in case they offend it;
instead they call it
'the old man in the fur coat'.

Human pollution has caused
the average length of
polar bears' penises
to shrink.

A male polar bear will follow
the tracks of a breeding female
for more than 60 miles.

Spiny anteaters
form 'love trains' where
a female is followed for weeks
by a line of ten hopeful males.

'Esperanto' means 'hopeful'
in Esperanto.

One in ten lottery tickets in Turkey
is bought from a single kiosk
with a reputation for
selling to winners.

In 2010,
exactly the same numbers
came up in the Israeli lottery
twice in three weeks.

Four is the only number
whose value is the same
as the number of letters
in its name.

Multiplying 21978 by 4
reverses the order of the numbers.

MOW, NOON and SWIMS
read the same when upside down.

In 2010, Brazil, Russia, India and China
invited South Africa to join
the BRIC group of nations.
They would have asked Nigeria,
but BRICS made a better acronym.

The acronym 'lol'
was being used in the 1960s
to mean 'little old lady'.

The Korean version
of 'lol' is KKK.

More than half of all Koreans
are called Kim, Lee, Park,
Choi or Jung.

Jung's grandfather
taught his children Hebrew
so they would be able to read
the newspapers in heaven.

In the 1720s,
the *Gloucester Journal* apologised for
'the present scarcity of news'
and offered its readers
a selection of poems instead.

Kinmel Hall in Wales
had a room that was used for nothing
but ironing the daily newspapers.

Royal household staff
iron a £5 note every Sunday
so that the Queen has something
to put in the church
collection plate.

The Union Jack
only flies over Buckingham Palace
when the Queen is *not* there.

The British subjects who
are happiest in their work
are gardeners and florists.

A *ziraleet* is
an outcry of joy,
especially by several people at once.

Strikhedonia is the joy of
not giving a damn.

Ataraxia is
complete freedom
from stress and anxiety.

John Le Carré
has a poster
in his study that reads
'Keep Calm and Le Carré On'.

Abraham Lincoln
calmed himself down
during the American Civil War
by playing marbles.

Stressed koalas
suffer from a fatal condition called
'wet bottom'.

A koala's brain
is only 0.2% of its
body weight.

The smallest known brain
in a healthy person belonged to
Anatole France, winner of the
1921 Nobel Prize for Literature.

We have more brain cells
as a newborn baby
than we will ever have again.

There are 100 trillion atoms
in a human cell
and 100 trillion cells
in the human body.

50,000 cells in your body
have died since you
started reading this sentence.

The murder rate in the UK
is 11 people per million;
in Cabot Cove, the setting for
Murder, She Wrote,
it's 1,490 per million.

In Germany, *Murder, She Wrote*
is called *Mord ist ihr Hobby*
('Murder Is Her Hobby').

Man-eating tigers
almost always attack people
from behind.

In 23 movies,
Dolph Lundgren has
killed a total of 662 people.

Jagdish Raj, holder of
the Guinness World Record
for 'most typecast actor',
played a policeman in 144 movies.

The world record
for keeping a kite aloft
is seven and a half days.

The world shorthand record
was set at 350 words a minute in 1922
and has never been beaten.

In 2010, a British man
spent 121 days in a room with 40 snakes,
only to be told that Guinness no longer
maintain the world record he was
trying to break.

A rattlesnake
that has been out in the rain
will not rattle.

Birds can't burp.

Mice can cough.

A crocodile cannot
move its tongue.

'Jimber-jawed' means
having a protruding lower jaw.

A jaguar's jaws are strong enough
to bite through a turtle's shell.

A Panamanian termite can
close its mouth at more
than 150 mph.

Adolf Hitler bit his nails.

Kooteninchela deppi
is an insect fossil
with triple-pronged claws,
named after Johnny Depp in
Edward Scissorhands.

Sylvilagus palustris hefneri
is a rabbit named
after Hugh Hefner.

Phialella zappai
is a jellyfish named after
Frank Zappa
because its discoverer
wanted to meet him.

The real names of the
Marx brothers were
Leonard, Julius, Herbert and Adolph.

Until the late 17th century,
pine cones were known as
'pineapples'.

The word *barack*
is Hungarian for 'peach',
Hebrew for 'flash of lightning'
and Swedish for 'shed'.

Britons spend
60 million hours a week
in their sheds.

One in ten
National Lottery millionaires
bought caravans with their winnings;
one in four
bought hot tubs.

St Mungo,
the patron saint of Glasgow,
died of shock after
getting into a hot bath.

St Nicholas
resurrected three small boys
who had been cut into pieces
and pickled in brine.

The medieval French made up their
own saints, such as St Coquette,
the patron saint of talkative women,
and St Jambon, the patron saint of ham.

Pope John Paul II,
who held office for 26 years,
created more saints than all the popes
in the previous 500 years.

When Pope John Paul II
visited California, the Hollywood sign
was changed to read 'Holywood'.

The Golden Palace Casino in Texas
bought Pope Benedict XVI's
old VW Golf
on eBay.

According to the Vatican,
you can reduce the time
you spend in purgatory
by following the Pope
on Twitter.

The word *papa*
means 'pope' in Italian,
'shark' in Swahili, 'potato' in Quechua
and 'arse' in Maori.

The Italian name for @
is *chiocciola*, meaning
'snail'.

The Dutch name for @
is *apenstaart*, meaning
'monkey's tail'.

The Danish name for @
is *snabel-a*, meaning
'"a" with a long nose'.

The Czech name for @
is *zavináč*, meaning
'pickled herring'.

The Manx word for 'kipper'
is *skeddan jiarg*,
which literally translates
as 'red herring'.

The word 'jungle'
comes from the Hindi *jangal*,
meaning 'waste ground'.

The Thai word for 'tapir'
is *P'som-sett*, meaning 'mixture',
because tapirs look as if they are
made up of bits left over
from other animals.

The 'slush' in 'slush fund'
was originally leftover fat
that sailors sold for profit.

In the 1790s,
a quarter of the sailors
in the Royal Navy
were black.

The modern British army
has more horses
than tanks.

American citizens
own more assault rifles
than the British army.

You can join the army at 16,
but you have to be 18
to play *Call of Duty*.

In an average
three-hour game
of American football,
the ball is in play
for just 11 minutes.

In 2011, the UK's top-selling
single in cassette form
was *N Sync's 'I'll Never Stop'.
It sold a total of 11 copies.

The Basque word for '11'
also means 'infinite'.

$$111,111,111 \times 111,111,111$$
$$=$$
$$12,345,678,987,654,321.$$

The Irish language
has one set of numbers for arithmetic,
one for counting humans
and one for counting non-humans.

Bees can count
up to four.

Wasps can recognise
each other's faces.

Octopuses can be
taught to open jam jars,
but will have forgotten how
by the next day.

During Isaac Newton's
29-year fellowship at Cambridge,
he taught only three pupils.

Handel wrote
the 259-page score of *The Messiah*
in 24 days.

The longest anyone
has gone without sleep is
18 days, 21 hours and 40 minutes.

The medical condition
known as a 'stroke'
is short for
'a stroke of God's hand'.

North Carolina, Arkansas, Maryland,
Mississippi, South Carolina,
Tennessee and Texas
all ban atheists from
holding public office.

You need a licence
to sell seaweed in England.

Under the UK's Salmon Act of 1986,
it is illegal to handle salmon
in suspicious circumstances.

Honking your car horn,
except in an emergency,
is illegal in the city
of New York.

Only 1% of car alarms that go off
are caused by an attempted theft.

When working as an organist,
Puccini stole and sold the pipes
and then changed the harmonies so
no one noticed the missing notes.

Charles Dickens's brother Frederick
was imprisoned for debt
and died an alcoholic.

Dickens nicknamed
three of his children
Flaster Floby, Lucifer Box and
Chickenstalker.

Coyotes
can run faster
than roadrunners.

A coyote
crossed with a dog
is called a 'coydog'.

A cross between
a zebra and a pony
is called a 'zony'.

Chemshebongo,
the Swahili for 'crossword',
means 'boil-brain'.

The world's largest jigsaw
has 552,232 pieces.

The official state sport
of Maryland
is jousting.

The official state dance
of North Carolina
is the Shag.

The largest-ever Irish dance
involved 10,036 people,
and took place in
Dublin, Ohio.

The cancan
was originally a dance for couples
and its earliest stars
were men.

'Hip-hop'
first appeared
in English in
1672.

Winston Churchill's mother
had a tattoo of a snake
on her wrist.

King Charles XIV of Sweden
had a tattoo which read
'Death to Kings'.

400,000 human beings
are born every day.

In June 2013,
21 women born
in the 19th century
were still alive,
but no men.

The average temperature
of a beehive
is the same as that
of the human body.

There is 40 times
more energy in empty space
than in matter.

Iceland is the
world's youngest land mass;
Greenland is the oldest.

If we could extend
our lives indefinitely,
we'd still die, but in an accident,
at an average age
of 1,200.

An 'endling'
is the final
individual in a species.

Eugene Cernan,
the last man to walk on the Moon,
wrote his daughter's initials
in the lunar dust.
They will still be legible
in 50,000 years.

A Note on Sources

For anyone keen to verify any of the facts in the book, they can be found online by going to qi.com/1339 and typing the relevant book page number in the search box. There is also a wealth of additional background detail about much of the information. Please do let us know if you have a quibble or a correction and add your own discoveries via our Twitter account @qikipedia.

The three people credited with compiling these facts are not the only ones who deserve the credit for it. Particular thanks are due to the core research team of Anne Miller, Andrew Hunter Murray, Anna Ptaszynski and Alex Bell, the miners of many more tons of factual ore than the book was able to carry. They were supported by the wider QI family: Rob Blake, Will Bowen, Stevyn Colgan, Mat Coward, Jenny Doughty, Piers Fletcher, Chris Gray, Molly Oldfield, Justin Pollard, Dan Schreiber, Freddy Soames, Liz Townsend and Richard Turner. And, as ever, the book's first and best editor was Sarah Lloyd.

Thanks are also due to Faber, our esteemed publisher. If patience is nature's secret then Stephen Page, Julian Loose, Eleanor Crow, John Grindrod, Hannah Marshall, Paula Turner and Anne Owen already have it cracked.

Index

This is here to help you find your favourite bits.
Like the facts themselves, we've kept it as simple as we can.

antlers 231; Antoinette, Marie 194, 199; ants 131, 132, 294; appendixes 257; applause 163, 164; Apple, Inc. 38, 267; apples 287; apricots 188; Arabic 52, 73, 109, 286; archaeology 186; arguments 164; Aristotle 304; armadilloes 71; Armenia 118, 173; armies 39, 125, 253, 270, 273, 325; armpits 52, 205; arms 55, 178, 179; arse-wisp 19; art 102, 103, 118, 236; ash 84, 271; aspirin 146, 167; assassinations 181; astatine 227; astronauts 8, 22, 66, 134, 203, 227, 251; atheism 329; Atkins, Dr 264; atomic bombs 239, 264, 287; atoms 263, 314; audiences 117, 163, 164; 'Auld Lang Syne' 152; Austen, Jane 143; Australia 75, 107, 146, 215, 249, 279, 250, 251; avocados 32, 33; Azerbaijan 57

babies 3, 4, 44, 59, 62, 105, 137, 157, 164, 199, 266, 267, 314; Babylon 286; Bach, Johann Sebastian 245; bacteria 2, 3, 91, 101, 168, 288; baked beans 114, 115; balls 209, 278, 326; Bangladesh 202; Bank of England 302; bankers 99; banknotes 2, 301, 302; bankruptcy 98; banks 1, 139, 280; *barack* 320; Barbie 156; Barcelona 209; baseball 209; Basque 326; bathroom 104; baths 40, 57, 204, 237, 253, 321; bats 85, 173, 276; batteries 256, 303; battles 5, 17, 53, 179; beaches 36, 75, 272; beards 16, 192; bears 3, 4, 82, 146, 147, 290, 307; Beatles 48, 200; beauty 214; beds 60, 205, 214, 297; beehive 334; beer 34, 183, 191, 192, 279, 286; bees 15, 16, 132, 160, 327, 334; Beethoven 163, 199, 245; beetles 25, 263; Belarus 164; Belgium 47, 251; Bell, Alexander Graham 196; bells 152; Ben & Jerry 264; Bentham, Jeremy 234; Berlin, Irving 163; Beyoncé 141; Bible 18, 116, 127, 128, 161; Bic 39; bicycles 109, 151, 300; Bierce, Ambrose 247; bimbos 56; birds 15, 21, 35, 77, 110, 134, 206, 244, 266, 317; Birmingham 23; birth 75, 87, 133, 300, 334; birthdays 67, 68, 244; biting 24, 73, 136, 249,

friendship 216, 264; frogs 133, 185; frost 180; fruit 45; fuel 146; funerals 196; fungi 206; fur 200, 201, 307

Gaelic, 216; Galilei, Galileo 68, 177; gambling 154; games 50, 78; Garden, Lady 249; gardening 312; gas masks 39; GCSEs 98; gender 11, 84; genes 220; genitals 42, 276; geology 145; Geordies 31; German 33, 238, 252; Germany 34, 78, 99, 105, 243, 260, 315; germs 261; Geronimo 62; Gershwin, George 48; gestures 153; ghosts 28; Gilbert and Sullivan 164; ginger beer 198; giraffes 289; Glasgow 44, 169, 321; glasses 172; gloves 251; goats 205, 271; God 18; gold 144, 145; Goldberg, Whoopi 104; gold rushes 145; Goldilocks 155; golf 11, 12, 31, 67, 278, 282, 299; Golightly, Holly 94; Google 66, 277; Grand Central Station 196; grass 108; *Grease* 297; *Great Gatsby, The* 149; Greece 289; Greenland 229, 335; greetings 288; grenades 193; guillotine 20, 184; guinea pigs 110; Guinness 192; Guinness World Records 271, 316; gullible 213; gunpowder 188; guns 22, 23, 290, 325; Guy Fawkes 47

haemorrhoids 2; hagfish 170; hair 29, 30, 160, 200 249, 305, 306; ham 321; hamsters 109; Handel, George Frideric 199, 328; hands 55, 200, 282; handstands 130; hangovers 41; Hannibal 125; happiness 312; harps 139, 185; harpsichords 20; #hashtags 193; hatred 125; Hawaii 244; headaches 42; heads 171, 189, 272; health and safety 249; heart attacks 43, 66; hearts 43, 54, 66, 129, 259; heaven 310; Hebrew 310, 320; hedgehogs 71; Hefner, Hugh 319; height 53, 95, 161, 212, 218, 225, 246, 251, 256; Heinz 114, 115; Hendrix, Jimi 199; herrings 323, 324; Heyerdahl, Thor 208; hiding 122; Higgs boson 229; Himalayas 4; *Hindenburg* 252; Hindi 324;

hip-hop 333; hippos 295; Hiroshima 239, 264; Hitchcock, Alfred 156; Hitler 5, 50, 318; holidays 195, 244; Holly, Buddy 172; Hollywood 322; Holmes, Sherlock 166, 221b; homelessness 280; honey 132; hope 308; horses 53, 91, 325; hospitals 74, 119, 249; hot tubs 320; house arrest 280; House of Commons 28, 135; House of Lords 249; Hughes, Emlyn 100; Hugo, Victor 103; hula-hoops 179; human body 32, 43, 53, 54, 63, 76, 101, 106, 137, 145, 161, 206, 218, 314, 334; humming 76; humour 203; hurdles 208; hurricanes 266; husbands 128, 295; Huskies 65; Hussein, Saddam

IBM 278; Ibsen, Henrik 289; ice 229, 230; Ice Age 231; ice cream 232, 264; Iceland 335; idiots 159; IKEA 114; illegal 1, 2, 80, 123, 151, 154, 250, 255, 299, 329; imitations 235; immune system 300; indexes 198, 339; India 78, 147, 149, 309; Indian 92; Indonesia 151, 203; infinity 326; information 277; injuries 109, 139, 249; ink 99; insecticides 9; insects 141, 319; insomnia 328; insults 112; insurance 117, 214, 281; Internet 173, 267, 268, 277, 323; intestines 179; intoxication 146; Inuit 126; invasions 120, 257, 298, 299; inventions 19, 20, 38, 39, 60, 78, 79, 148, 219, 259, 270, 288, 291; invertebrates 110; iPhones 267; Iran 80, 91; Irish 51, 327, 332; ironing 311; irony 283; islands 75, 159, 203, 211, 272; Israel 308; Italian 238, 322, 323; Italians 18, 237

Jaffa Cakes 97; jaguars 318; jails 50, 255, 280, 330; jam 327; January 195; Japan 55, 171, 232, 233, 237; Japanese 56, 89, 296; jaws 318; jazz 282; jeans 140, 151; Jedi 28; jellyfish 113, 319; Jenga 78; Jesus 48, 129; jewels 122; jigsaws 332; jobs 29, 260, 281, 282; John O'Groats 83; Johnson, Amy 22; jokes 203; journalism 236; journeys 14, 234; jousting 332; Judaism 116;

Jung, Carl 50, 310; jungles 324; Jupiter 138; *Jurassic Park* 275

K2 212; Kabul 120; Kafka, Franz 281; Kalashnikovs 114;
Kama Sutra 169; kangaroos 75, 187; karaoke 251; kayaks
126; kebabs 165, 274; Kent 211; Kentucky 50, 212; Kentucky
Fried Chicken 188; Kenya 81; kestrels 224; Ketamine 73;
ketchup 114; kettles 36, 37; Kevins 266; keyboards 261;
Keynes, John Maynard 197; keys 282, 288; kidnapping 118;
kidneys 80; killing 13, 53, 72, 74, 128, 168, 221, 224, 233, 242,
287, 315; kilts 159; kimchi 186; kingfishers 269; kings 16,
17, 27, 36, 40, 122, 159, 166, 173, 174, 194, 254, 260, 289, 295,
333; Kipling, Rudyard 113; kippers 324; kissing 80, 81, 193;
Kitchener, Lord 289; kites 316; kitty litter 124; kiwis 207;
knees 57; knights 175; Knights Templar 80; knives 217;
koalas 313; Komodo dragons 293; kookaburras 269; Koran
129; Korea, North 36, 151, 186, 296, 310; Korea, South 36,
186, 296, 310; Korean 87, 238, 310; krill 107; Kubrick, Stanley
154; Kuwait 130

Labour Party 28; lacrosse 247; lakes 64, 112, 113, 250, 291;
lamps 185; Land's End 83; landfill 108; landscapes 250;
language 3, 35, 92, 110, 111, 116, 117, 128, 174, 202, 216, 243,
252, 273, 295, 308, 322, 323, 324; Laos 111, 274; lasers 115;
Latin 3, 216, 240; laughter 164; Laurel and Hardy 105;
lava 138; laws 23, 141, 212, 235, 243, 250, 253, 255, 286, 299,
306, 329; lawyers 33, 281; Le Carré, John 313; lead 145; Lee,
Bruce 12; left-handed 55; legs 60, 61, 88, 140, 142, 200; letters
153, 267; libraries 169; lies 198; lifts 225; light 83, 134, 162;
lighters 252; lightning 70, 320; Lightyear, Buzz 157; Lincoln,
Abraham 181, 281, 301, 313; lions 72; literature 149; livers
32; llamas 302; lobotomies 161; lobsters 189; locusts 225;

lol 310; lollipops 288; London 14, 25, 26, 40, 49, 50, 81,
87, 158, 175, 195, 199, 267; London Underground 40, 158;
Long John Silver 142; look 13, 49, 101, 216, 261, 300, 324;
Lord Byron 197; *Lord of the Rings* 5; lorries 219; losing 287;
lotteries 308, 320; Louvre 26, 103, 261; love letters 153; LSD
285; luck 66; Ludo 78; lunches 157; Lundgren, Dolph 315;
lungs 54, 63

Macbeth 159; mace 203; magnets 229; magnolias 31; Major,
John 260; malaria 233, 301; Malaysia 233; Maldives 152;
malnutrition 265; Malory, Thomas 280; Manchester 257;
Manchester United 209; manners 16; Manx 324; Manx
shearwater 15; Maori 322; marbles 313; Marianas Trench
24; markets 120, 174, 274; Marmite 219; marriage 85,
86, 183, 258, 295, 300; Mars 53; Martini 198, 283; Marx
Brothers 319; Marx, Harpo 139; Marx, Karl 100, 254; Mary
Queen of Scots 12; Maryland 329, 332; mass 228, 229;
masturbation 231; maths 326; mating 59, 291, 295, 308;
matter 228, 334; Mayans 105, 195; meals 2, 37, 127, 216,
293; measles 270; measurements 7, 58, 234, 263; meat 6,
127, 201; medals 126; *Mein Kampf* 5; melting 229, 230;
memory 32, 121, 327; Mengele, Josef 80; Merkel, Angela
257; Mexicans 272; Mexico 23, 24, 87, 297; mice 89, 233,
317; Michelangelo 68, 102; Mickey Mouse 258; midges 46,
88; military 17, 73, 120; milk 6, 90, 91, 291; Milky Way 263;
millipedes 110, 140; Milton, John 154; minerals 202; minimum
wage 257; Missouri 213; mistakes 181; mistletoe 288; mobile
phones 119, 196; *Moby-Dick* 35, 61; Mohammed 129, 175;
moles 46, 271; moments 194; *Mona Lisa* 103, 261; money
122, 139, 154, 257, 286; monkeys 72, 288, 289, 323; monks
294; monsters 171; Moon 49, 138, 226, 251, 335; moose 231;